# MILITARY CUSTOMS
## AND
## TRADITIONS

*By the same author*

COMPANY DUTIES

BATTERY DUTIES

HANDBOOK AND MANUAL FOR THE NONCOMMISSIONED
OFFICER (editor and contributor)

ARMY LORE AND CUSTOMS OF THE SERVICE

# MILITARY CUSTOMS
# AND
# TRADITIONS

by

## Major Mark M. Boatner III

Illustrated by Lieutenant Colonel Lachlan M. Field

GREENWOOD PRESS, PUBLISHERS
WESTPORT, CONNECTICUT

Library of Congress Cataloging in Publication Data

Boatner, Mark Mayo, 1921-
    Military customs and traditions.

    Reprint of the ed. published by D. McKay Co., New
York.
    Bibliography:  p.
    1.  United States.  Army--Military life.  2.  United
States.  Army--History.  3.  Military ceremonies, honors,
and salutes--United States.   I.  Title.
[U766.B58  1976]      355'.00973        75-17189
ISBN 0-8371-8299-9

Originally published in 1956 by David McKay Company, Inc., New York

Reprinted with the permission of David McKay Company, Inc.

Reprinted in 1976 by Greenwood Press
A division of Congressional Information Service, Inc.
88 Post Road West, Westport, Connecticut 06881

Library of Congress Catalog Card Number 75-171189
ISBN 0-8371-8299-9

Printed in the United States of America

10 9 8 7 6 5 4

For

Stirling and Bruce

# Acknowledgments

To Mr. Fairfax D. Downey (author of *Indian Fighting Army, Mascots,* etc.) I am indebted for professional literary guidance.

To Colonel Frederick P. Todd (author of *Soldiers of the American Army, Cadet Gray,* etc.; Editor of the *Military Collector and Historian;* Curator of the West Point Museum, and probably the country's leading authority on U. S. Army lore) I am grateful for many pleasant hours of expert assistance.

Thanks to Mr. C. C. Soden of Australia, a lifelong student of military origins, for the barrage of valuable material with which he responded to my call for help.

Mr. C. E. Dornbusch of the New York Public Library, who has long pursued the thankless task of collecting unit histories, gave me much material help and moral support.

Colonel Elbridge Colby (author of *Army Talk*) was kind enough to help with the chapters on military lingo.

Lt. Col. James G. Chesnutt, Chief of the Army's Magazine and Book Branch, PID, gave me official assistance above and beyond the call of duty.

For typing, appreciation is expressed to Miss Jane O. Mathey, Miss Irene Knihnicki, Miss Adrienne M. Donlon and Mrs. Esther M. Bell.

Thanks to the staff of the West Point Library for getting me off-the-trail books, and for not sending me very many overdue notices.

My biggest debt of gratitude is to my father, Colonel Mark M. Boatner, Jr., for whatever intellectual curiosity I may possess— and no hard feelings for passing down more of his curiosity than his intellect.

# Foreword

You might expect a professional soldier to start a book like this with a long blast on the *importance* of military customs and traditions. I will refrain. Not because I don't feel strongly about it, but because the effort would probably be wasted.

I would like to point out, however, that this field has been neglected in our country. To my knowledge, this is the first attempt in America to deal with the entire subject in a single book. While I make no excuses, I know I have rushed in where the real authorities apparently have feared to tread.

This is a small book not because the material is limited (there is a two-volume work on uniform buttons alone!), but because I want it to appeal to the general reader. My problem was not in finding things to put in this book, but in deciding what to leave out.

When some real military scholar gets around to giving the subject the definitive treatment it deserves, I will be the first to applaud. In the meantime—and we have already waited a century and a half—*Military Customs and Traditions* is for the civilian as well as the person in uniform. Out of consideration for the reader whose interest is more than casual, I have tried to cite references and authorities, but not at the expense of readability.

I would be grateful for suggestions, material and "leads" into the field of military Americana. Mail will always reach me at this address.

M. M. B.

PENRITH PLANTATION
JACKSON, LOUISIANA
    March, 1956

# Contents

# Illustrations

# MILITARY CUSTOMS
## AND
## TRADITIONS

# CHAPTER 1

# How Armies Evolved

SOLDIERING, the world's third oldest profession, is heir to a tradition that stretches back to the dawn of mankind. The one element that has varied least through the ages is the soldier himself.

"Centuries have not changed human nature," wrote Ardant duPicq.[1] "Passions, instincts—particularly the most powerful instinct of self-preservation—these things are expressed differently in accordance with the times, the circumstances, the character and temperament of races. . . . But, beneath it all, the same man is to be found."

America is in the process of developing its own distinctive military system, its own brand of soldier, "in accordance with the times, the circumstances, the character and temperament of races." But we have not "invented" the American Army. We have inherited, borrowed and stolen. We have bought with blood. We have tempered with the fires of victory and the chills of adversity.

The future will tell how good the American product is. But to visualize our military future we must know something of its past.

## British Heritage

Our Army, like most of our other national institutions, is patterned closely after the British. Emory Upton [2] notes that even our traditional civilian apathy toward the military is an Anglo-Saxon heritage. Because of American indifference toward military history

[1] Colonel Ardant duPicq, *Battle Studies* (Harrisburg, Penna.: Military Service Publishing Company, 1921). First published in Paris, 1880.
[2] General Emory Upton, *The Military Policy of the United States* (Washington, D.C.: 1917).

3

we must turn to foreign pens for first-rate accounts of our own heritage.

One of the most remarkable sources is the late Sir John W. Fortescue, historian of the British Army. He gives the following explanation of early military origins.[3]

### How the First Military Company Was a Commercial Company

In about the fourteenth century, when firearms began to appear on the field of battle, "there grew up mercenary bands of professional soldiers in Switzerland, Italy and Germany, whose leaders would accept contracts to fight for or against anyone. These bands were known as companies, and were, in fact, formed on a commercial basis, men of substance investing money according to their means in the buying and equipping of recruits, and taking rank according to the amount of their investment. The profits which they hoped to make consisted of plunder and of ransom for wealthy prisoners; and, when weary of the profession, they sold their shares in the company to anyone who would buy.

"The companies varied in strength from tens to hundreds, and even thousands, and the symbol of their corporate existence was their flags or colours by which they set great store, especially among the German bands. If by chance any disgrace fell upon a German company, the colours were furled, planted upside down in the ground, and not flown again until the culprits responsible for the crime had been tried and punished by an assembly of the whole company. It is from these companies that fifes (German: *pfeif*, meaning pipe) and drums (Oriental instruments brought to Europe by returning Crusaders) and many of our military terms are borrowed. . . .

"From the German companies we derive our reverence for the colours, the firing of three volleys (in the name of the Trinity) over the dead. . . ."

The mercenary system reached its best developed form in Italy. Intense economic rivalry among the rich trading republics (Venice, Milan, Florence, etc.) made it necessary for each to have its own army. Services of English and Swiss fighters were particularly

[3] John W. Fortescue, *The Empire and the Army* (London: Cassell and Co., Ltd., 1928). Quoted with permission.

sought after. (The Swiss Guard of the Vatican are a vestige of the
ancient Free Companies.)

Most military terms are, therefore, derived from the Italian. The
French invaded Italy in 1494, picking up the basic military words
(e.g., infantry, cavalry, colonel, battalion, regiment) and passing
them on to the rest of the world.

### The First Standing Armies

Near the end of the fifteenth century the French king raised
*companies* of men-at-arms (*gens d'armes*). These were the first
permanent regular forces to be organized since the fall of Rome.
The units were composed of armored horsemen, foot archers and
halberdiers (of whom his Scottish Guards were the elite).

### The German *Landsknechte* and *Reiter*

The origin of modern military organization can be traced to the
German *Landsknechte* (Infantry) and *Reiter* (Cavalry) which developed in the latter part of the fifteenth century. They were modeled
on the fourteenth-century Italian *Condottieri,* the Swiss mercenaries
and the English *Free Companies.* By the end of the sixteenth century the regimental organization of the *Landsknechte* and *Reiter*
had been generally adopted by all other European armies.

The first country to possess a formidable standing army was
Spain in the sixteenth century.[4] During the same century, France,
the Holy Roman Empire and the Netherlands followed suit. Sweden,
England and Prussia raised large standing armies in the seventeenth
century.

In the following period of Continental wars, developments in
organization were brought about by the great military reformers.
Successful armies became the model for other countries. The first
innovator was Maurice of Nassau, who led the Dutch in their bloody
struggle to drive Spain from the Low Countries toward the end of
the sixteenth century. Gustavus Adolphus, King of Sweden, about
this same time developed an army that was unbeatable during the
Thirty Years' War.

[4] The nucleus of this "formidable standing army" was four trained infantry regiments whose combined strength was only 7,000!

*Landsknechte* and *Reiter,* from whom most of our "modern" ideas of military organization stem.

## ORIGIN OF MODERN MILITARY METHODS

Within this brief outline of "modern" military history, it's now possible to take a look at how most of our twentieth-century military usages came about. You are probably wondering why the Roman and other even more ancient armies did not have more influence on present traditions and customs. Why are we going back only as far as the fourteenth century? The answer is that military knowledge died in the Dark Ages along with other forms of knowledge. Dead was the Roman Legion, which Oman [5] referred to as "that wonderful combination of strength and flexibility, so solid and yet so agile and facile to maneuver."

Warfare emerged from the Dark Ages as a natural manifestation of the feudal system. As Oman put it, "The epoch is, as far as strategy and tactics are concerned, one of almost complete stagnation; . . ." Infantry had all but disappeared; it was the day of the mail-clad horseman.

The basic "combat unit" at this time was the "Lance." It consisted of the fully armored knight with his retinue of squire, page and three or four mounted retainers. But it was apparently impossible to "organize" these Lances. Due to personal vanities and the peculiar chivalric code that placed the premium on personal exploits of valor, each knight fought in a tactical vacuum. Such a basic concept as maintaining a reserve was out of the question; no self-respecting knight would sit quietly on the side lines during the first stages of the battle while others copped all the glory.

The English archers, Genoese crossbowmen and the Swiss halberdiers then began to come onto the battlefield. This spelled the end of the knight on horseback. He was "dead" after the battle of Crécy (1346); but he did not lie down and die until *Don Quixote* administered the coup de grâce (1604).

[5] Oman, C. W. C., *The Art of War in the Middle Ages,* revised and edited by John H. Beeler (Ithaca: Cornell University Press, 1953). This standard reference was first published in London in 1885 and expanded in 1924 to two volumes.

## EVOLUTION OF ARMY ORGANIZATION

The first "companies," as we've seen, were of no prescribed size. Practice soon showed, however, that they should be reduced to a number that one commander could handle in action. Since 100 men was about as many as could be controlled by voice, this became the standard size.

### How the Regiment Came into Being

An *administrative* organization was needed to control the companies (which were *tactical* formations). So they began to be collected into groups under the rule or *regiment* of a single officer who was called the *colonel.*

The regiment bore the name of the man who raised it or who succeeded in its command. This practice continued down to the nineteenth century, although *numbers* began to replace *names* in the eighteenth.

The colonel retained command of his original company. His second-in-command was the next highest ranking company commander, who, likewise, retained command of his company. In his new capacity, the second-in-command was the staff officer of the regiment and had the title of *sergeant-major.*

Since the colonel was often absent from the regiment—protecting his interests in court or simply taking advantage of practically "owning" the regiment to be AWOL—a *lieutenant colonel* was needed to run the show. His title literally means "taking the place of the colonel."

### Why a Lieutenant General Ranks a Major General

Now we have the clue to a minor military mystery. When Cromwell's "New Model Army" was raised in 1645, it was commanded by *Captain General* Sir Thomas Fairfax. The cavalry (being the "senior service") was commanded by *Lieutenant General* Oliver Cromwell and the infantry was under *Sergeant Major General* Skippon. That's why a lieutenant general ranks a major general. The rank we now call "major" was originally "sergeant major."

## Origin of Other Titles

The company was normally formed tactically into a *squadra* (square) at the head of which was a reliable veteran who became known as the *capo di squadra* ("head of the square," not "squarehead"). This title comes to us as "corporal" from the French *caporal*.

Sergeant comes from the Latin *servire* (to serve). During the days of chivalry the term *serviens* was applied to fighters who were a cut above the common soldiers, yet who were not wealthy enough to qualify as knights. They were, however, mounted. If one lost his horse he became known as a *lanz spessado* (broken lance); he joined the foot soldiers where he acted as a noncom and was known as a lance sergeant or lance corporal.

Captain comes from the Latin *caput* (head) through the Latin *capitaneus* (chief).[6] Although he could logically be the head of *any* unit, since early in the history of armies he has commanded the company-size unit (a battery in the artillery and a troop in the cavalry and, now, in Armor).

"Lieutenant" comes from the French *lieu* (place) and *tenant* (holding). He is one who "holds the place (job) of" another. Although we have the ranks of Lieutenant Colonel and Lieutenant General, the "Lieutenant Captain" is called simply "lieutenant."

"The word colonel," Fortescue explains, "is a puzzle. It may be derived from 'columna,' a column, or 'corona,' a crown. It used to be spelled indifferently 'colonel' or 'coronel'; and we have solved the problem by spelling it in the first way and pronouncing it in the second."

In Chapter 3 we'll see the origins of other military words.

## DEVELOPMENT OF THE "COMBAT ARMS"

Armies are composed of "combat arms" which do the actual fighting and "supporting services" which back them up administratively. The "Arms" in a modern army are Infantry, Armor and Artillery. The "Services" are Quartermaster, Medical, Ordnance,

---

[6] J. T. Shipley, *Dictionary of Word Origins* (New York: The Philosophical Library, 1954).

Chemical, Transportation, Engineers,[7] Signal,[7] Chaplains, Military Police and the Adjutant General's Corps.

## "Queen of Battles"

Infantry was the "Queen of Battles" in ancient warfare and still is today. With the decline of the Romans, however, Infantry supremacy died. It was almost a thousand years before Infantry was again the decisive arm.

During the feudal epoch, the man on horseback ruled the battlefield. Foot soldiers were, for the most part, ragged mobs of unkempt, undisciplined, poorly armed soldiers who just couldn't afford to buy a horse and equipment.

In the fourteenth century all this began to change. At Crécy and Poitiers, English archers clobbered the cream of French chivalry. Swiss halberdiers gave the same treatment at Morgarten and Sempach to Austrian horsemen. During the next century the Swiss phalanxes—having replaced their halberds with pikes— defeated the Burgundian Horse at Morat and Nancy to assure Swiss independence. In Bohemia, the blind Jan Zizka—a rare tactical genius—organized the Hussite peasants into an unbeatable infantry force that was able to destroy the elite Austrian cavalry.[8]

Within the general designation of "infantry" there have been many different kinds of "soldiers who fight on foot."

The first battalions were composed of musketeers and pikemen in varying ratios. As muskets became more effective, the pikemen— whose function it was to protect them from cavalry—were reduced. Finally they formed such a small group as to be called a *picquet* or "little body of pikes," from which comes the modern term "picket" or outpost.

Grenades (from *grenada,* pomegranate) were introduced during the Thirty Years' War (1618–48). Particularly tall, powerful men were selected from each battalion to throw the "hand-bombs" and became known as "Grenadiers." Later they were formed into spe-

---

[7] Sometimes classified as "combat arms," since their mission frequently requires them to fight with the three "combat arms."

[8] Zizka's infantry was closely supported by artillery and cavalry. For this he is credited with inventing the concept of "combined arms."

cial companies, one per battalion, and given the position of honor on the right flank. In some cases they were further assembled into regiments, like the "Grenadier Guards" in England and designated elite units. "Grenadier" continued to be the term for elite troops long after their function had ceased to exist in battle.

A fourth variety of infantry came into being during the seventeenth century when the light flintlock musket or *fusil* was developed. They were (logically enough) known as Fusiliers.

The need for select troops of superior mobility and with special weapons has always been apparent in battle. The Italians employed "skirmishers" (from *scherma,* fencing) as early as the battle of Pavia in 1525. This type of troops was eventually known as Light Infantry. In the course of centuries the Light Infantry function has been performed by Grenadiers, Fusiliers or by special units with the specific designation of "Light Infantry." At one time each battalion of the American Army was composed of ten companies; eight were "battalion companies," while the two flank companies were designated "Light Infantry" companies. (See page 89.)

Frederick the Great, in the eighteenth century, was given a great deal of trouble by a species of guerrilla troops known as the Austrian Light Infantry. Frederick adopted the idea and formed his own Light Infantry. Then he went a step further and organized special units of foresters and gamekeepers which he called *Jäger* (literally "huntsmen"). The French followed suit in 1759 and formed a Corps of *Chasseurs* (the French word for "huntsmen"). In 1805 the French also raised light units of small, agile men called *Voltigeurs.*

British reverses at the hands of American Indians and backwoodsmen led them to revive their concept of special elite infantry units. A "Corps of Light Infantry" made the march from Boston to Lexington and Concord to touch off the "shot heard round the world." It was a "Corps of Grenadiers" that assaulted Bunker Hill.

During the Napoleonic Wars, Light Infantry was employed a great deal. Since then, however, the designation, like the terms Grenadier and Fusilier, has been used only in the honorary sense.

A purely American type of special infantry troops are Rangers. Used during the French and Indian Wars and the Revolution, they were revived during World War II and Korea. Parachute Infantry is another variety of elite infantry troops in existence today.

## Cavalry

In ancient times Cavalry was a very subordinate arm. It was not until the development of the stirrup that a man on horseback could use weapons in a manner that made him a serious menace to disciplined foot troops.

Chinese literature first mentions the stirrup in 447. After 528 it is referred to several times in Chinese and Korean writings.[9] It seems to have appeared in Europe around 550. Although authorities are wary of giving the date it was "invented," they seem to agree that it started as a simple loop fixed to the end of the saddle skirt. Even the most confirmed pedestrian will understand, however, that without stirrups the man on horseback can be considered nothing more than a nuisance in battle. With both hands free to handle a weapon, he becomes something to contend with.

True Cavalry can hardly be considered to be descended from the mounted knights of old. The latter fought on horseback with great dash and for centuries after the fall of Rome ruled the battlefield. But they were not organized so as to provide the disciplined shock action and maneuverability that characterize Cavalry.

The German *Reiter* (or *Ritter*) of the early sixteenth century were the first "modern" Cavalry. They were organized almost exactly in the same manner as the *Landsknechte*. (See page 5.)

*Reiter* units raised by captains were called *troops* rather than *companies*—a distinction carried into Cavalry organization of the twentieth century. Several troops formed a *squadron. Reiter* squadrons were composed of six ranks having a front of fifty men; this size was determined by the number of men who could be effectively commanded in battle by one leader. Gustavus Adolphus preserved the same frontage but reduced the number of ranks to three (total, 150 men).

Although the early *Reiter* were unarmored (as shown in our illustration), it was not long before they started wearing helmets and cuirasses (covering the upper part of the body). This armor

[9] Young, Captain J. H. A., "Chinese Weapons of War," *Australian Army Journal,* April, 1955.

was black, a distinction which made the *Reiter* known throughout Europe as the "Black Riders." Their weapons were the pistol and the sword.

Three general types of Cavalry eventually developed and were used for several hundred years: Heavy Cavalry (or *Cuirassiers*); Light Horse (e.g., Hussars, Lancers); and *Dragoons.* The latter were really mounted infantry; they were armed with a large firearm—called a "dragon," because it appeared to be spurting flame from its mouth—and dismounted to fight.

Frederick the Great was the originator of true Cavalry tactics. His troopers were not permitted to fire from the saddle. He developed units capable of high speed over long distances and trained them to charge "boot to boot in long lines of scores of Squadrons. The training and tactics of Frederick's Cavalry have never been improved on, and are still the model for shock action," wrote Foster just before World War I.[10]

Barbed wire and machine guns sounded the death knell of the gallant Cavalry in World War I. However, the last American horse Cavalry (First Cavalry Division) was not dismounted until 1943. A strong argument can still be made for the use of horse Cavalry on special operations in modern war. (Russian Cavalry in World War II is estimated at 300,000.)

### Engineers and Artillery

Modern Engineers and Artillery, whose functions in battle are now entirely separate, can trace their lineage to a common source: the King's *Ingeniator,* a high official mentioned in English history as far back as William the Conqueror (1066). The *Ingeniator* had charge of all "engines" (Latin *ingenia*) of war.

About 1300 this official became known as *Atillator.* The change was brought about when artillery was added to his collection of "engines of war." (This man was known in English as the *Engyneor,* a term derived from the French *Engineur.*)

Artillery was not a separate arm of the service until the seventeenth century. Until then, guns were just a portion of the field trains accompanying the army. As late as the eighteenth century

[10] Colonel Hubert Foster, *Organization* (London, 1913).

these guns were moved by civilian teamsters on contract. They were escorted by Infantry, whose original mission was not so much to protect them as to keep them from running away!

The weapons were worked by a Master Gunner with a Gunner and two assistants for each piece. These lads were highly specialized technicians who commanded very fancy wages for their services. They earned their pay, however. One occupational hazard was the fact that guns frequently blew up and killed the entire crew. Moreover, their long-range weapons were considered unsporting—even by such fearless and irreproachable generals as the Chevalier Bayard; captured gunners were more likely to be executed as "war criminals" than given the honorable status of prisoners of war.

Bearing out the French theory that *"Plus ça change, plus c'est la même chose"* (the more things change, the more they remain the same), American engineers and artillery were once combined into a common "arm." In 1794 the "Corps of Artillerists and Engineers" was created; it consisted of two regiments which existed until 1802. This represents an organizational throwback of eight centuries to the time when the King's Ingeniator commanded both artillery and engineers.

It is also interesting to note that while artillerymen were originally civilians, the military engineer existed centuries before the civilian engineer. The civil engineer is a nineteenth-century by-product of his military counterpart. Until fairly recent years, most important civil engineering tasks in this country were accomplished by Army engineers.


## DEVELOPMENT OF THE "SERVICES"

### Adjutant General

The office of Adjutant General was created in the British Army late in the seventeenth century. He was concerned with personnel and with routine matters not connected with operations or logistics. During the intervening 250 years, the AG's duties have changed very little.

Being charged with the publication of orders and recommending administrative policy, the Adjutant General got to be the real power

behind the commander. In the early part of this century, when
Secretary of War Elihu Root was insisting on long-needed army
reforms, the then AG (Ainsworth) put up such a howl about the
incroachment on *his* authority that the threat of court-martial had
to be used to bring him into line.

### Chaplains

Priests have accompanied most armies. They may have actually
*led* some prehistoric forces into battle.

There is a story that Richard Coeur de Lion was the first to use
military chaplains. During the Crusades when he was having trouble
making his conscripts give their all for Christianity, Richard is
alleged to have assigned a priest to each body of troops to arouse
their martial ardor. This early military chaplain appears to have
combined the tasks of lead scout with those of Troop Information
and Education Officer. Before the battle he threatened malingerers
with eternal damnation. Then he led them into battle with his cross
held high. The conventional cross is even said to have been modified
to make it a more effective instrument of hand-to-hand combat: a
spike was put on one end and a heavy knob on the other.[11]

Chaplains disappeared from military organizations during the
fifteenth century. Cromwell, however, brought them back into military service in the New Model Army. Although no longer required
to lead attacks, Cromwell's chaplains were required to know how to
dress wounds.

### Medics

Up until the sixteenth-century German mercenaries, no doctors
accompanied military units. During the wars of the Middle Ages
the sick and wounded were left to make out as best they could. If
they got any attention it was from private citizens who took pity
on them, or from monks who, in those days, were the only people
who knew anything about medicine or surgery.

A surgeon was assigned to each company or troop of the *Landsknechte* and *Reiter* (page 5). When the practice of surgery
passed from the hands of the monks to those of barbers, the change
was reflected in the seventeenth-century military organization of the

[11] C. C. Soden, "How It Began," *Australian Army Journal*, June, 1955.

Prussians: *Feldschere* ("field barbers") were attached for surgical duties (Foster). The present-day red-striped barber pole is a symbol from the days when barbers were *supposed* to cut more than hair.

## Military Police

It may be that Military Police were created to perform the same function for which Marines were first used—to protect the officers from their men!

According to C. C. Soden,[12] recruiting methods reached intolerable extremes in 1740 to replace heavy casualties in Flanders. The "pressed men" took advantage of any opportunity to express their aversion to military life by knocking off an officer. Trustworthy soldiers were selected to protect officers' quarters and to guard them against ambush on the way to work.

A century later when the original need had disappeared, the "Watch Guards" were reorganized and assigned a true "military police" role. The office of "Provost" was then created to control them.

## Quartermasters and Logisticians

The office of Quartermaster goes back to the sixteenth-century *Reiter* (page 12). His original job was to find quarters and rations for the men. In connection with the first duty, the "quarter-master" of necessity had the function of reconnaissance.

In sixteenth-century France, an officer known as *le Major Général des Logis* was charged with just about all the duties now performed by the entire General Staff.[13] As recently as 1870 the Quarter Master General (QMG) was the second officer to Moltke on the Prussian General Staff.

Each man foraged for himself during the early European wars when armies could "live off the land." When pickings became slim, a centralized system was organized for collecting supplies from the local inhabitants and storing them for issue to the troops. It was

[12] *Op. cit.*

[13] In the modern American Army the General Staff consists of four officers: G-1 (Personnel and Administration); G-2 (Intelligence); G-3 (Operations, Plans and Training); and G-4 (Logistics).

later found to be more efficient and to require fewer soldiers if the army bought its supplies from the locals. Since money was involved, this put the supply system under the Civil Finance Department in the British Army.

A Transportation Service was then required to move supplies from rear depots to the combat units. Until the nineteenth century, supply trains were handled by "Civil Service." Due to the great reluctance of these businessmen to furnish their services within range of gunfire, they soon had to be replaced by soldier drivers under the command of army officers.

In this pattern of soldier-to-civilian-to-soldier control of combat "services" there is a lesson for moderns. Soldiers have never shown much aptitude for "business methods"; businessmen, on the other hand, have never shown much stomach for soldiering. A common meeting-ground is yet to be found.

"Logistics" is considered a very modern word for the business of supplying soldiers. Actually, it is an ancient term which has come back into vogue after several centuries of disuse. "Logistics" once meant *all* staff duties (from the fact that, as we noted above, the *Major Général des Logis* originally performed *all* staff functions).

## EVOLUTION OF WEAPONS

Man first fought like any other animal: with his hands, feet and teeth. He discovered early that a fist was more effective if it held a rock or stick. Early wizards soon realized that certain *selected* rocks and sticks were better than ones picked up at random. The armament race was on.

The object of fighting has always been to defeat or drive away the enemy while keeping yourself a maximum distance from him. (This is as true today as ever.) Our ancestors therefore looked for ways to increase the range of weapons. Rock throwing must have been the first development in this direction. Then a stone was tied to a piece of vine or leather thong, whirled and let loose. This increased range but decreased accuracy; the science of "exterior ballistics" was born; brains began to emerge over brawn as the prerequisite for survival.

Slope-browed survivors of early "meeting engagements" soon

learned that weapons could be classified as offensive and defensive. Early man probably devoted more "thought" to providing himself with a satisfactory club for close-in protection than he did to the perfection of his rock-slinging style.

The club must have been the weapon man first *made* for himself. The sling, the spear and the stone ax probably followed in roughly that sequence. The shield certainly occurred to somebody fairly early in the game.

But a characteristic of armaments races is that as soon as a new weapon is developed to give its user an advantage over the foe, there are always enough survivors of the first defeat to steal the idea and use it in turn against its inventor.

So along came the early refinements of the basic club and thrown stone. Men learned to chip flint so that stones could be shaped into stronger and more effective ax heads. Throwing sticks were developed to give spears more range; arrowheads and spearheads were fashioned. The bow was invented.

Around 5000 B.C. it was found that a certain kind of rock could be hammered into desired shapes. About 2,000 years later a piece of this rock happened to get next to a fire and a little pool of bright liquid formed. Copper had been discovered and began to be used for weapons. Later some tin accidentally got mixed in with a batch of copper and the result was bronze. It was more difficult to work, but it took a real edge and was much harder than copper. (It is still an important metal in weapons, particularly for cartridge cases in which role it played a vital part in the development of breech-loading and repeating weapons.)

Progress in the development of weapons was restricted for centuries to improvements in the basic prehistoric arms. The tremendous and ingenious war engines of the Romans and of the Middle Ages—the catapult, ballista and battering ram—were really nothing but "improved" slings, bows and clubs.

### Gunpowder

The next big development was gunpowder, which appeared in the beginning of the fourteenth century. Various *incendiary* compounds such as "Greek fire" had been used since the dawn of history, but we must not confuse them with *explosive* compounds.

Oman [14] devotes ten pages to the invention of gunpowder and cannon. Roger Bacon seems to deserve credit for the discovery of gunpowder—an *explosive* mixture of saltpeter, sulphur and charcoal. He wrote about it in 1249. Bacon, however, did not anticipate the use of his invention in cannon but merely to make "flying fire" and for psychological effect on the enemy (particularly his horses). "But gunpowder . . . was known for over sixty years before its propulsive power was discovered, and utilized to throw missiles," Oman says.

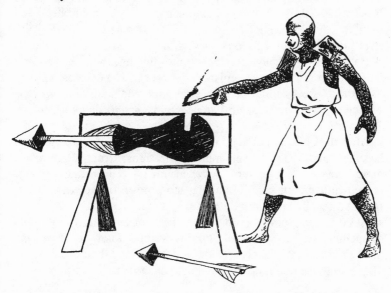

The first picture of a true cannon (based on an illuminated manuscript dated 1327 in the library of Christ Church, Oxford)

A sort of early-day mortar—called a *madfaa*—is described in an Arabic manuscript as having been used in about 1304. The earliest picture of a gun is in a manuscript dated 1327. A vase-shaped affair about four feet long, it is shown shooting a heavy arrow at a castle door. "But from 1325 onward there is no disputing the existence of cannon all over Western Europe, which gradually developed from

[14] Oman, *op. cit.*, vol. II, pp. 205–214. (Reference here is to 1924 edition.)

their original impractical shape into something like modern weapons," concludes Oman.[15]

Gunpowder's main use in fourteenth-century warfare was in huge cannon to knock down the walls of fortresses and cities.

## Handguns

"The ancestor of the musket and rifle was a toy cannon strapped to a pike handle," Oman writes.[16] Italy took the lead in their development. The early handguns were not as effective as the longbow. Not until 1420 did they evolve into something that could be aimed from the shoulder. The Hussites (in what is now Czechoslovakia) were the first to use them on a large scale.

Handguns gradually developed into the hackbut, caliver and musket. Eventually they replaced the longbow, not because they were more effective, but because a recruit could acquire reasonable proficiency with them faster than he could learn to shoot a longbow accurately.

After the invention of gunpowder, the evolution of weapons again became a matter of relatively minor perfections: stronger gun tubes, more manageable handguns, better means of transporting artillery, breech rather than muzzle loading, more powerful powder, invention of a recoil mechanism, etc.

Almost every new weapon since the slingshot has been hailed as spelling the "end of civilization as we now know it." Even the most skeptical must concede, however, that since the advent of the "Big Bang" the doom-criers may have something.

## Flintknapping: a Link with Antiquity

A handful of men are engaged today in an art that has existed for at least 2,000 years in the vicinity of Brandon, Suffolk County, England. Theirs is the trade of "flintknapping": the chipping of flint.

The same quarries that yielded this special type of stone for pre-

---

[15] Oman convincingly discredits the theory that the German monk Berthold Schwartz discovered gunpowder in 1313—"he comes thirty or forty years too late to claim the credit of being the first gunner." Oman, vol. II, pp. 211, 214.

[16] Oman, *op. cit.*

historic tools and weapons are now producing the material from which Atomic Age workmen, using Stone Age know-how, are supplying gun flints for flintlock devotees in America.

"Britain's oldest industry" reached its peak between 1686 and 1835 when Brandon was the center of the gun flint making business. (According to Funk & Wagnalls' *New Standard Dictionary*, the flintlock was invented in Spain in about 1625, superseding the matchlock; the percussion-lock was invented about 1840, making the flintlock obsolescent.)

For about a hundred years the Brandon flintknappers kept their hand in by supplying gun flints and flints for fire-making devices to the less enlightened parts of the world. Finally even these last markets were destroyed by civilization in the form of breech-loading rifles, safety matches and Zippo lighters.

A new demand for gun flints has arisen during the last few years. It has become apparent that ancient war surpluses in this item have been nearly used up.

At last report,[17] about four flintknappers in Brandon are working part time to replenish the world's dwindling stock pile of gun flints.

[17] Arthur Woodward, "Some Notes on Gun Flints," *Military Collector & Historian*, June, 1951. Don't be misled by the expression "some notes"; this is a long, illustrated article by an expert.

## CHAPTER 2

# Pomp and Pageantry

### Uniforms

MILITARY uniforms, in the sense we know them today, have been worn only during the last three hundred years.

Prior to the seventeenth century, soldiers conformed to the civilian dress of the time and were distinguished only by their military arms and equipment.[1] Not until the eighteenth century did closeness of fit begin to distinguish military attire from civilian.

The armies of the old Roman Empire did not wear a true uniform. They did, however, present a somewhat uniform appearance by virtue of having helmets, body armor, shields and weapons of a more or less standard design.

In England during the reign of King John (thirteenth century) it became the custom to wear a loose sleeveless surcoat which was put on over the mail shirt and extended to the knees. In the next century, under Richard II, English soldiers wore the red cross of St. George sewn on the front and back of their white canvas surcoats to identify them in battle. By the end of the fifteenth century, recruits in England were being given an allowance for "coat money" (in addition to the "conduct money" to cover their travel to join their units). With this, according to Fortescue, the soldier bought a white coat, "probably a canvas smock with the red cross of Saint George sewn upon it from collar to skirt."

But authorities seem to be in general agreement that the household troops of Louis XIV (seventeenth century) were the first to

---

[1] An exception was the leather jacket which was popular during the Thirty Years' War.

22

be fitted out in what could be called a uniform in the present sense of the word. By 1700 almost all soldiers (in Europe) wore uniforms.

The oldest uniforms still in existence are those worn by the Papal Guard of the Vatican (said to have been designed by Michelangelo) and those of the "Yeomen of the Guard," raised by Henry VII in 1485.[2]

The first purpose of a military uniform is, of course, to distinguish between friend and foe. A second consideration, in the early days, was strictly one of economics: in foreign countries the colonel was responsible for clothing his regiment and it was cheaper to buy the material in bulk lots. Until fairly recent years, each U. S. regiment had its own uniform. An act of Congress in 1792 prescribed that soldiers "shall be uniformly clad in regimentals, to be furnished at their own expense; the color and fashion to be determined by the brigadier commanding the brigade to which they belong."

It was Cromwell, in his organization of the New Model Army (mid-seventeenth century), who first recognized the value of uniforms in promoting unit pride.

In his *British Military Uniforms*, James Laver lists three principles governing the development of all costume, including military:

1. The "Seduction Principle." By widening the shoulders, narrowing the hips and increasing his apparent height (shakos, bearskins, etc.), the soldier is made to look more masculine. The original purpose may have been to frighten the enemy. In modern times it plays an important part in recruiting; girls have always tended to look longer at a man in uniform than one in civvies.

---

[2] A note for nit-pickers. Some authorities say Henry VIII raised the "Yeomen of the Guard" in 1510 and the "Yeomen Warders of the Tower" in 1519. I suspect that certain military genealogists have traced the lineage of the first unit back to the older royal bodyguard of Henry VII. Soden points out that the term "Beefeater" cannot properly be applied to the Yeomen Warders of the Tower (of London). Both units wear the same red uniform with the exception that the Yeomen of the Guard also have an embroidered shoulder belt (originally used to support the arquebus). Only the latter unit, whose mission it is to guard royal residences at Windsor Castle, Whitehall Palace, etc., are properly called "Beefeaters." See Chapter 3 for origin of the word "beefeaters."

2. The "Hierarchical Principle." This establishes social position and in the Army is reduced to distinction of military rank.

3. The "Utility Principle." Laver points out that this has as little influence on military dress as it has on civilian!

### The *Fourragère* and Aiguillette

These are horribly un-American words for common items of military ornamentation worn in all armies. You have undoubtedly seen them—metal-tipped, colored cords worn around the shoulder. The aiguillette is the mark of an aide de camp. The *fourragère* is awarded as a unit citation. There is some disagreement as to whether the *fourragère* is a separate item of ornamentation, or merely a form of aiguillette.

Let me say right now that nobody really knows how these items originated. The distinguished military historian Fortescue declines even to make a guess.[3]

Here are some of the prevalent theories:

The aiguillette, as the badge of an aide, has been traced to the picket lines carried by squires to tie out the knights' horses; to the metal-tipped thongs used by the squires to lace knights into the early types of armor; to the pencil carried on a string by aides ("adjutants") for writing down orders. What all these theories have in common is that they account for the metal tip and are associated with aides or adjutants.

Perhaps there is a clue in the word itself. *Aiguille* is French for "needle." Modern French meanings of *aiguillette* include "metal-tipped thong." If we can infer a meaning of "needle" rather than "nail, pencil tip," etc., from the word itself, then we arrive at one set of conclusions. Perhaps the item evolved from the needle carried by musketeers for cleaning out the touch holes of their weapons. If so, what is its association with aides?

The *fourragère,* as a unit citation, has been traced by some to a

---

[3] This refers to his comments following a lecture by Major C. T. Tomes on "Military Customs Still Extant," printed in the *Journal of the Royal United Services Institution,* vol. 70, London, 1925. This out-of-the-way source has proved to be one of the most valuable I have come across. Further reference will be to "Tomes," or "Fortescue comments on Tomes lecture."

hangman's rope and a nail! One story is that a unit (Duke of Alva's Flemings?) was threatened with mass hanging if they did not start doing better in battle. They exhibited their self-confidence by providing the equipment. Naturally, their next operation was such a success that the ropes were retained as a "unit citation."

Another yarn is that a general (Cromwell?) threatened to hang any member of a particular (Irish?) regiment he ever captured. The regiment showed its (Irish!) contempt by providing the equipment.

Still another story (and we might as well have all of them) comes from the Franco-Prussian War (1870). The Paris jails were cleaned out to form provisional units for the defense of the city. One group wrapped hangman's ropes on their shoulders as a sort of improvised insignia. They performed so well that they were kept in service after the war and permitted to keep their "insignia."

Again, the word itself furnishes a clue. *Fourragère* is still used in French to describe "fodder" or "forage." Parties sent out foraging might logically have carried ropes around their shoulders for tying up bundles of forage.

The *fourragère*.

Having exhausted the curiosity of most readers as to the origin of words they had probably never heard anyhow, we will now leave the subject. For those who are interested in what I consider the "last word" on the *fourragère* and aiguillette, I invite your attention to Appendix A, p. 163.

### Origin of Sashes

The sash may be an item of ornamental equipment that once had a functional purpose: to improvise litters for carrying wounded off the field. This theory seems to stem primarily from James's *Military Dictionary* (1802) and has been widely repeated. Edwards points out that the sash has been traced back to the seventeenth century, at which time it was a cumbersome silk affair which was wide enough to carry a man.

However, there is every indication that the sash—merely a variation of the scarf—was first and last an item of ornamentation. It may have been *used* to carry wounded, but was hardly *invented* for that purpose.

While the sash was at one time worn by private soldiers (it was a distinguishing feature of the seventeenth-century Pikeman's dress), it later became a badge of military office. When swords were carried only by gentlemen and common soldiers, the former wore sashes for identification.

West Point is the only place in the American Army today where the sash is still worn. It identifies cadet officers and certain others when acting in an official capacity.

### Batons and "Swagger Sticks"

Fortescue says he has traced the Field Marshal's baton back to an "ordinary bludgeon." He believes "it must have been confined to the Teutonic people and copied by the French." [4] Most authorities agree that the Marshal's baton is but a variation of the Sovereign's mace which, in turn, has been traced back to the sacrificial ax of prehistoric times. [5]

"Swagger sticks" evolved from the "leading cane" prescribed for British officers in a General Order of 1702. On parade this cane was used for leading the men. But it was also used for administering on-the-spot punishment of up to twelve strokes for minor violations of regulations. (Examples of the latter were "Sneezing in the ranks, scratching the head, or giving his officer a cross look.") [6]

The term "swagger stick" is self-explanatory. British officers and soldiers of some units carry them when off duty. Sometimes the riding crop was carried by mounted personnel.

Despite the American prejudice against military show, "swagger sticks" appear from time to time with official sanction of local commanders. Not only do they satisfy a human desire for something

[4] Fortescue comments on Tomes lecture, *op. cit.*

[5] F. Britten Austin, *A Saga of the Sword* (New York, 1929) and others.

[6] C. C. Soden, "Army of Yesterday" series in *Mufti*, the Australian veterans' magazine, September 1954–June 1955.

to occupy the hands, but they also help combat that horrible and most unmilitary tendency of putting your hands in your pockets.

### Chevrons

The word *chevron* is French for "rafter." As often happens, however, the French Army today uses another word, *galon* ("stripe"), where we use the word "chevron."

When the practice was started of decorating shields, the problem soon arose of how to achieve the necessary variety. Since all primitive design makes use of straight lines and geometric patterns, the earliest variations were the cross; the "bend" (a diagonal stripe from the shield's upper right to its lower left—one going the other way was the "bend sinister," symbol of illegitimacy); the "bar" (a horizontal stripe); the "pale" (a vertical stripe); the "saltire" (a diagonal cross or "**X**"); a checkerboard pattern; and a chevron (two lines or stripes meeting at an angle).

When a simple but distinctive sleeve device was needed to indicate rank, the chevron was undoubtedly appropriated from heraldry.

Inverted gold chevrons were used by the British Army up until 1830 to denote the rank of officers. They ranged in number from one for second lieutenants to eight for full generals. (Soden)

Chevrons appear to have come into the American Army by way of the West Point cadet uniform. In 1817, Colonel Sylvanus Thayer, then Superintendent, ordered that cadet officer rank be shown by a complicated system of chevrons worn on the sleeve. In a year this system was scrapped for a more complicated one. (Variation was achieved by turning some chevrons upside down, and wearing them on different parts of the sleeve.) This system, in effect until 1820 at West Point, passed into the rest of the Army; between 1821 and 1832, captains and lieutenants as well as noncommissioned officers wore chevrons. (Captains wore one chevron *above* the elbow; lieutenants wore one *below* it.)

Since 1832, only noncoms have worn chevrons in the American Army, except at West Point, where they are still used to show the rank of cadet officers as well as cadet sergeants and corporals.[7]

[7] Information on American use of chevrons is from F. P. Todd's *Cadet Gray* (New York, 1955).

## Epaulettes and Shoulder Straps

During the time of Queen Elizabeth (1558–1603), shoulder straps were introduced in the form of leather thongs which were tied around belts to keep them in position. It was not long before they began to get more and more elaborate.

Officers of the "trained bands" (militia) wore shoulder knots of plain brown leather. But officers of Queen Elizabeth's personal staff were soon sporting elaborate articles of red and gold silk braid.[8]

Shoulder straps were retained as a distinctive but purely ornamental feature of U. S. officers' shirts until after World War II. Now they are worn by all ranks.

"The origin of epaulettes is mentioned in the 'Lives of the Lindsays,'" Fortescue reports.[9] "As far as I can make out, the officers wore bundles of ribbons simply for ornament." Lace was also worn in the same fashion.[10]

## Origin of Khaki

The word "khaki" means "dust-colored." First worn in India by British troops during the Afghan War (1878–9), it originally was white drill dyed with curry powder [11] or colored with dust or mud. This "field expedient" arose from the need to give British soldiers some camouflage against dead-eyed native marksmen.

Radford gives the following interesting account in his *Unusual Words.*[12]

The origin of the khaki uniform of the British soldier is told here for the first time from information given by Mr. J. Leeman, son of the inventor. In 1883, Mr. J. Leeman was travelling in India for a Manchester cotton firm. A Colonel Kinlock suggested to him that he could acquire a fortune if he could produce a cotton drill, khaki-coloured, which would be fast to the sun and to washing. At that time some regiments in India were dipping their white uniforms in mud as

[8] Soden, *op cit., Australian Army Journal,* June, 1955.

[9] Fortescue comments on Tomes lecture, *op. cit.*

[10] See also pages 89–91, "Evolution of Rank Insignia." For those interested in a more esoteric treatment, see "American Army Epaulettes 1814–1872," by Mendel L. Peterson, *Military Collector & Historian,* March, 1951.

[11] Tomes, *op. cit.*

[12] Radford, *op. cit.* Quoted with permission.

a means of concealment. Back in England, Mr. Leeman approached a Lancashire dyer, Mr. F. A. Gatty, and together they carried out experiments. Samples were prepared and were boiled by Mrs. Leeman in a copper pan. When dried in the sun, however, the colour faded. More samples were prepared for test. On this occasion, however, the copper pan was cooking the dinner, so Mrs. Leeman boiled the cloth in an old rusty pan. This "did the trick," as the dye used (oxide of chromium) was fastened by the oxide of iron from the rusty pan. A private company, F. A. Gatty and Company, Ltd., was formed, and has since clothed the troops of the British Empire for more than a half a century.

### Buttons

Distinctive buttons have long been a feature of military uniforms. There is some evidence to support the theory that one of the original purposes of ornamental buttons was to keep soldiers from wiping their noses on the sleeves of their dress uniforms. (Mothers make a note.)

In the British Army, the precedence of "Guards" regiments is symbolized by the spacing of buttons down the fronts and on the cuffs of their dress tunics. The senior unit, the Grenadier Guards, spaces the buttons singly. The buttons of the Coldstream Guards are worn in pairs to indicate that they are officially considered to be the second oldest unit.[13] Buttons of the Scots, Irish and Welsh Guards are arranged in threes, fours and fives, respectively, in accordance with their relative seniority.

The size of U. S. Army buttons is designated by the "line" (*ligne*)—40 "lines" to the inch. All officers except those of the Corps of Engineers wear gold-colored buttons on their service coats ("blouses"). These buttons are 36-line (down the front of the blouse) and 25-line (on pockets). They bear the coat of arms of the United States. Enlisted men's buttons are of the same size and design, except for 45-line buttons on overcoats, but are made of olive-drab plastic. (Officers wear plain buttons on their overcoats.)

The distinctive button worn by Engineer officers shows an eagle flying off with a scroll in its beak bearing the Engineer motto

---

[13] Actually, they are the senior regiment. See page 50.

*"Essayons"* (literal translation, "Let's try"). A bastion and rising sun are in the background.

### Haversacks and Packs

The modern pack dates only from 1745. Up until this time the European soldier—unlike his overloaded twentieth-century descendant—had no requirement for a haversack or pack. He was not even issued an overcoat until fifty years later.

According to Lawson, the "Guards" regiments were the first to be issued a pack. It was a cowhide bag, made so that the hair faced outward, and worn slung on the back. The haversack, made of gray canvas, was worn on the right side in much the same way as our Army used to wear the "musette bag." Water bottles were issued at the same time.

As for overcoats, these were announced as an item of issue about 1795 in the British Army. Prior to this time, about twelve "watch coats" were provided for each regiment; they were what we would today call "guard property" and were reserved for wear on sentry duty.

The derivation of the word "canteen" is covered in Chapter 3 (page 55).

### Hair

Soldier haircuts in the early days conformed to civilian styles. Some military modifications must have been made in those times as today, however, to accommodate the type of hat or helmet then being issued.

Early in the eighteenth century, the British soldier was ordered to start wearing his hair in a queue (French, "tail"). This called for saturating the hair in tallow, packing it into a solid mass, and tying it with a black ribbon. The whole mess was then powdered with ordinary flour! Thus treated it could never be washed. Conditions resulting from this silly convention are best left to the reader's imagination.

The French Revolution brought about changes in men's hair and clothing styles. The American Army abolished the queue in 1801 along with knee pants and other fashions associated with non-republican foreigners. Napoleon did away with long hair and the queue in the French armies around 1806; as a mark of honor, however, he permitted his Old Guard to keep their old-fashioned coats and their long hair. The British Army started eliminating the queue in 1790; in 1808 the War Office issued an order that all pigtails would be cut off, and then countermanded it. But by the time "Change 1" caught up with the order, not a head of long hair remained in the British Service.

An interesting British military tradition resulted from the elimination of queues. When the latter were prescribed, a small patch of black leather was ordered sewn on the back of the jacket to protect the uniform from this greasy, rancid appendage. The Royal Welch Fusiliers were stationed at Quebec when the change in hair style was ordered. By some oversight they were not told that the black patch was also to be removed. When they returned to England several years later they fought for and obtained authority to retain the patch. They wear the black ribbon "flash" today.

### Beards and Mustaches

Military fashions in chin whiskers have varied considerably throughout history. As in all other military styles, civilian customs of the time exert considerable influence.

The ordinary Roman legionary was clean-shaven, in contrast to the shaggy barbarian. But Roman officers and veteran soldiers wore beards as a sort of distinctive marking.

Feudal warriors were usually bearded and whiskers were the professional soldier's trade-mark during the Renaissance.

Beards went out of fashion around 1700. They were retained as the distinguishing insignia of certain special troops like sappers (field engineers or "pioneers").

Until fairly recent times, military beards and mustaches were governed by a rigid protocol. Mustaches were prohibited in the British Army until the early 1800's. But the British were so impressed by Polish lancers at Waterloo that in 1817 they converted some of their own light cavalry into lancers and hussars. In so doing they copied the Polish and Hungarian prototypes not only in uniforms and tactics but also to the extent of prescribing their mustaches. If a trooper couldn't grow one he had to use paint and artificial hair! The "cavalry type" mustache is traditional even today.

The American Army started a losing battle in 1835 to stop the import of foreign fashions in mustache styles. In 1840 an official exception was made that "Officers and men of the dragoons [mounted infantry] are permitted to wear mustachios of a fashion to be regulated by the Colonels of their respective regiments." The rest of the Army, however, continued blithely to ignore official injunctions against mustaches for "officers or men on any pretense whatever." The influx of bearded and mustached Volunteers for the Mexican War further frustrated the writers of General Regulations in Washington. Since 1843 the subject of hair had been "specifically directed" to the attention of all officers; the words *short* and *cropped* had been pointedly italicized in the regulations.

Yet we emerged from the Civil War with two of the hairiest armies the modern world has ever seen.

"No horse, no wife, no mustache" is still the rule at West Point. But in the rest of the Army there is nothing that prohibits mustaches, sideburns or beards—so long as they are "short and neatly trimmed." [14]

### "Colors"

In the early Roman armies a company-size unit of 120 men was called a *maniple* ("handful"). It used a handful of straw on the end of a pole as a rallying point in battle. The *maniples* were later reorganized into *cohorts* (of three maniples each). At this time the straw standard was replaced by symbols such as bears, globes and dragons. Each legion had an eagle standard which was carried usually by a knight and was considered sacred. In later years each cohort had a square piece of cloth embroidered with its individual device.

During the Middle Ages, knights carried pennons or banners on the shafts of their lances for identification. We've already seen (page 4) that the earliest mercenary companies carried flags and considered them with great reverence.

[14] Most of this material is from F. P. Todd's "The Ins and Outs of Military Hair" (with 25 illustrations by H. Charles McBarron, Jr.) in the *Infantry Journal*, vol. XLVII, no. 2, March–April, 1940.

At about the beginning of the seventeenth century when armies were adopting the regimental system, it was decided to assign colors (using the word in its conventional sense) to each regiment. It was logical, then, for the "Red Regiment," for example, to carry a red flag for identification in battle. Hence military flags became known as "colors." [15] Another (slightly different) explanation of the term is that early heraldic flags bore the "colors" of a commander in precisely the same sense as used in horse racing today. (F. P. Todd)

On the other side of the world, in about 1650, the first of the Manchus was experimenting with a new concept of military organization. He divided his troops into four groups—the Yellows, Reds, Whites and Blues. Each was identified by a colored banner. Later he doubled the number of units, having each new unit take one of the original four colors and adding a border. [16]

In 1751 a British Army regulation prescribed that there would be only two "colors" in each regiment: the King's (or national) flag and the regimental flag. The Warrant of 1747 had prescribed that "no Colonel to put his Arms, Crest, Device or Livery on any part of the appointments of the Regiment under his command" and "that the second Colour [i.e., the Regimental flag] be of the same colour as the facings of the Regiment and to bear the Regimental Number." (The "facings" at this time were the lapels, cuffs and the turnback of the coat.)

So the "colors" originated as a means of battlefield identification and continued to perform this function for many years. The old rank of Ensign—originally an Army title, now existing only in the Navy—was assigned to the regiment's junior officer who carried the flag ("ensign") into battle. The color party marched into battle at the front and center of the regiment, so the casualties were high. Victories in the old days were expressed in terms of the number of enemy colors captured. Most acts of gallantry cited in orders were

[15] "We Englishmen do call them of late colours, by reason of the variety of colours they be made of...." From Richard Barrett's *Theorike and Practike of Modern Warres*, published 1589, and quoted in the *Journal of the Military Services Institute of the United States*, vol. 19, 1896.

[16] Captain J. H. A. Young, "Chinese Weapons of War," in the *Australian Army Journal*, April, 1955.

in connection with the defense or capture of colors.[17] The rank of Color Sergeant was introduced into the British Army in 1813 with a view to giving the Ensigns some local protection.

Being a Color Sergeant was a great honor and all that, but the soldiers of that day were realistic about it—there were times when they would just as soon not have the honor. Writing of Waterloo, a British sergeant said:

> About 4 o'clock I was ordered to the Colours; this, although I was used to warfare as much as anyone, was a job I did not at all like. But still I went as boldly to work as I could. There had been before me that day 14 sergeants already killed and wounded and the staff and the Colours almost cut to pieces.

The American Army conformed generally to British custom in the matter of colors until 1813. In that year the duty of carrying colors into battle was taken from Ensigns and entrusted to Color Sergeants. The Stars and Stripes was not carried as the national color until shortly before the Civil War. Instead, they carried a blue silk color on which was embroidered the arms of the United States, an American eagle bearing on his breast the shield and in his talons the olive branch and the arrows which signify peace and war. The regimental flags were of distinctive colors with the names of the units on them. After the change, the color with the eagle on it was made the organizational color, and the regiments were given the Stars and Stripes to carry as the second one. This system is still in effect.

Regiments and separate battalions are the only outfits that carry colors. Divisions have a distinguishing standard which shows the divisional shoulder-sleeve insignia ("patch"). Company-size units carry guidons (small flags) in the colors of their branches or arms.

The practice of carrying colors into battle persisted through the American Civil War; the last Medals of Honor awarded during this conflict were for capturing Confederate colors. In the British Army, colors were carried for the last time in battle at Laings Nek, 1881, during the first Boer War.

Modern armies now carry colors only in ceremonies. The Com-

[17] In 1950, the United States returned to Mexico the colors captured by our forces in 1846–1848.

munists in Korea would occasionally take a huge red flag into battle with the idea of planting it on a captured position for psychological effect.[18]

### Folding the Flag into a "Cocked Hat"

A distinctive American custom is that of folding the national flag into a triangular shape—stars showing—when it is lowered and taken off the staff.

The shape is supposed to represent the cocked hat of the American Revolution. The British and French have no prescribed ways of folding their flags.

### Why the British Colors Are "Trooped"

One of the most stirring ceremonies of the British Army is "Trooping the Color." It is the main feature of a ceremonial held annually by the "Guards Brigade" to mark the reigning monarch's birthday.

"Trooping the colors" has been traced to the days of the early mercenaries when men were taught to use their flag as a rallying point in battle. "Trooping" the colors before a battle assured that recruits would recognize them.

In eighteenth-century Britain, when military discipline was at a particularly low ebb, the colors were "trooped" at the periodic musters for an entirely different reason: to prove that they had not been misplaced. There are some amazing instances of colors being lost through neglect. In 1788, for instance, the colors of the Seventy-

[18] Here is an additional bit of modern American flag lore. As for nomenclature, the general term "flag" is used in the military service when no other more specific definition fits. A *color* is a flag carried by dismounted units, high commanders and certain general officers. A *standard* is a flag carried by mounted or motorized units. An *ensign* is flown on ships, small boats and aircraft.

The national flags flown from staffs on military installations come in three standard sizes. The largest is the *garrison flag* (38 by 20 feet); it is flown on holidays and special occasions (provided, obviously, that there is not much wind). The *post flag* (19 by 10 feet) is for general use. The *storm flag* (9½ by 5 feet) is used during bad weather; being the smallest of the three, it is also the one used to drape over caskets and for presentation afterward to the next of kin.

first Foot were left behind when the unit moved into another area in Northern Ireland; they showed up in 1921 in a Limerick pawnshop! Lawson tells of an officer of the Third Foot, entrusted with the regimental color, who was sick and left behind when the regiment moved. He died while billeted with a Devonshire farmer. The farmer kept the flag until many years later when he bequeathed it to the Royal United Service Institution, where it can still be seen. Sometime later the guidon of the Nineteenth Light Dragoons was lost for a hundred years.

### Battle Honors

The system of placing battle honors on the colors dates back to 1768 in the British Army. In this year, Eliott's Light Dragoons (later Fifteenth Hussars) were authorized to put the word "Emsdorf" on their helmets and guidons in recognition of their spirited action at that place. In 1784, four regiments were honored for their defense of Gibraltar by being authorized to place the word "Gibraltar" on their Grenadier and Light Infantry caps, their drums and accouterments, and on their colors.

During World War I some Germans wearing this British honor on their sleeves were captured! They belonged to units descended from Hanoverian regiments that had served with the British at Gibraltar and been awarded this honor. The badges were taken away from them in 1921 when the Reichswehr was inaugurated.[19]

In America, regiments were allowed to have battle honors embroidered on the stripes of their national colors in 1863. In 1890 this practice was abolished and the honors were inscribed on silver bands that were fastened around the staff of the regimental color. In 1920 we inaugurated the system of "battle streamers" showing the names of engagements and attached to the staff of the regimental color. The background color of the streamer varies for each war. Our most battle-tested regiment, the Seventh Infantry ("Cottonbalers"), has sixty streamers! Silver bands are still awarded to company-size units that are entitled to battle honors for actions they performed when not assigned to their parent unit. The Distinguished Unit Citation (a World War II innovation) is symbolized

[19] Major T. J. Edwards, *Military Customs* (Aldershot, England: Gale and Polden, 1950).

by a blue streamer, embroidered with the name of the action, which is also displayed on the regimental color.

There is a difference between "battle honors" and unit decorations, although both may be shown by streamers on the outfit's colors. The U. S. regiment with the most decorations is the Sixteenth Infantry. Its awards and those of two close runners-up—the Forty-seventh and Thirtieth Infantry Regiments—are listed in Chapter 4, page 108.

### Military Music

The drum is probably the oldest musical instrument. The first military music of real significance was the drum used in the Roman armies to beat cadence.

Marshal de Saxe [20] attributes the success of the Roman Legion to their fast foot marches and their system of battlefield control of troops by cadence marching. "There is the whole secret, and it is the military step of the Romans," wrote the great de Saxe in 1735. "That is why these musical marches were instituted, and that is why one beats the drum."

"The music of the legion consists of trumpets, cornets and buccinae," Vegetius tells us.[21] "The trumpet sounds the charge and the retreat. The cornets are used only to regulate the motions of the colors; the trumpets serve when the soldiers are ordered out to any work without the colors; but in time of action, the trumpets and cornets sound together. The classicum, which is a particular sound of the buccina or horn, is reserved for the commander-in-chief and is used in the presence of the general, or at the execution of a soldier, as a mark of his authority.

"The ordinary guards and outposts are always mounted and relieved by the sound of trumpet, which also directs the movements of the soldiers on working parties and on the field days. The cornets sound whenever the colors are to be struck or planted."

[20] Marshal Maurice de Saxe, *Reveries on the Art of War,* translated by Brigadier General Thomas R. Phillips (Harrisburg, Penna.: 1944).

[21] Flavius Vegetius Renatus, *The Military Institutions of the Romans,* translated in 1767 from the Latin by Lt. John Clark, British Army. The Military Service Publishing Company, Harrisburg, Penna., printed the book in 1944. Vegetius wrote in the fourth century.

The Swiss have been credited with "inventing" (in the fourteenth century) the practice of marching in step to fife and drum. In the next century this was copied by the *Landsknechte* and from them adopted by other armies. The roll of the drum that precedes the playing of a military march by British Army bands has been traced back to the old *Landsknechte* drum march.[22]

Real military "music"—as opposed to drums for beating cadence and horns for signaling—was developed by the Turks and Arabs. It was during the Crusades that European armies came into contact with Saracen music and were thoroughly terrified by it. The Saracens grouped musicians around their battle flag to mark its location in the dust of combat. So long as the Arab could hear the music above the clash of arms he knew that things were going all right. Minstrels brought back to Europe the new musical forms.

When the art of war was revived during the Renaissance, military companies began to include musicians. Trumpet and drum continued to be the principal musical instruments until the oboe arrived on the scene during the reign of Louis XIV of France. This marked the birth of modern military bands.

The bassoon and horn, the trombone and serpent, the trumpet and the clarinet were added to military bands during the next few centuries. In about 1840, the Belgian instrument maker Adolphe Sax produced his versatile family of "Saxophones" and military music was of age.[23]

The bagpipe is an ancient musical instrument which has existed in widely separated parts of the world. The Scottish "Ladies from Hell" in their swinging kilts and accompanied by their screaming "pipes" have been the terror of the modern battlefield as well as ancient ones.

America has made no contribution to military music that can challenge the acknowledged leadership of the French with their "Sambre et Meuse," "Madelon" and the "Marseillaise." John Philip Sousa, who died in 1932, has come the closest.

[22] Foster, *op. cit.*

[23] For information on the evolution of military musical instruments I am indebted to the United States Military Academy Band, West Point, N.Y.

### Bugle Calls

The bugle, short for "bugle horn," is a descendant of the hunting horn. The word "bugle" itself is an obsolete term for a wild ox or buffalo. The first hunting horns were unquestionably made from the horn of this animal.

As we've already seen, bugles were first used to control the movement of troops in battle. The armies of Gideon and Saul may have been the first to make military use of them.[24] The Romans are known to have used them in battle (page 37). Our encounter with the bugles of Communist enemies in Korea reminds us that certain primitive people still use them tactically—for control and for psychological effect.

Although ancient armies used bugles in battle, the instrument disappeared from military organizations during the Dark Ages. Bugles did not come back into military service until the Seven Years' War when German woodsmen and hunters were organized into military units (Jäger; see page 11).

"The curious thing is that the horn-signals of the chase right back in the 14th Century were very elaborate; and why they were not used earlier as signals for war I never could understand," said Fortescue.[25]

While bugles were absent from the battlefield their place was taken by drums for sounding signals. After bugles reappeared in battle, sometime near the end of the eighteenth century, their main function was to blow calls for regulating the day of soldiers who had no watches.

Regulation bugle calls for the British Army were written about 1793 by the great Austrian composer Franz Josef Haydn while he was in London on a working visit. It is interesting to speculate that some of our own calls may contain vestiges of his work.

Little is known about the origin of our own bugle calls. Probably we used British calls in the early days. Like the British, we had two distinct sets of calls: one for mounted troops and another for foot troops.

[24] William Carter White, *A History of Military Music in America* (New York: Exposition Press, 1944).

[25] Fortescue comments on Tomes lecture, *op. cit.*

White [26] gives the following foreign influences on American bugle calls. Reveille, Mess Call and the first eight bars of Tattoo are the same as the French *Reveille, Le Rappel* and *L'Extinction des Feux,* respectively. (Note, however, that in the case of Mess Call ["Soupy"] we use the call for a different purpose.) The second part of Tattoo (20 bars) is the British infantry "Tattoo, First Post."

Retreat and Reveille are believed to date back to the Crusades.

### Tattoo

How did a drummer's word like "tattoo" get tagged on a bugle call? It probably originated among the British troops in Holland during the Thirty Years' War (1618–1648) [27] or during the wars of King William III during the 1690's.[28] In any event, the word is derived from the Dutch *tap* (tap or faucet) and *toe* (to or off). When the time came for soldiers to leave the taverns and return to their billets, the Officer of the Day, with a sergeant and drummer, would beat his way through the streets. This was the signal for the Dutch tavern keepers (unless they wanted to be closed by the military authorities) to *"Doe den tap toe"* or turn off the taps.[29]

According to another theory, the word comes from the seventeenth-century German Army's *Zapfenstreich,* meaning "bung-line." The call had precisely the same significance as "tap toe." But the word itself came from the provost's fiendish practice of drawing a chalk line across the bungs of the barrels when he made his final evening check of the taverns; if his chalk lines showed any signs the next morning of having been tampered with, the innkeeper would be fined.[30]

References to "Taptoe" go back as far as 1701 in the British Army. Our own regulations of 1813 prescribe a roll call "at Taptoe time."

The call is now sounded at 9 P.M. in most units. It is the signal

[26] *Op. cit.*

[27] According to Edward Arthur Dolph, *"Sound Off"—Soldier Songs from the Revolution to World War II* (New York, 1942).

[28] The conjecture of Major T. J. Edwards, *Military Customs* (Aldershot [England]: Gale and Polden, Ltd., 1950).

[29] Edwards, *op. cit.*

[30] War Department, *Army Talk 184, "Customs of the Service"* (Washington, 1947).

to quiet down in barracks and to turn off lights within fifteen minutes. Some of our regiments used the call during the Mexican War
in connection with funerals.

## Taps

The music we now use for Taps has a most curious history.
Originally, the American Army used the French *L'Extinction des
Feux* ("Lights Out") for Taps. This call—said to have been Napo-
leon's favorite—did not suit General Daniel Butterfield, of the
Army of the Potomac.

Without knowing a note of music, General Butterfield undertook
to put together a call he considered more suited for signaling the
end of the day's activities. With the help of the brigade bugler
(Oliver W. Norton) the General created Taps one night in July,
1862, while in camp at Harrison's Landing, Virginia. It soon was
adopted by other corps and made official throughout the Army.

In 1932 the French Army adopted the American Taps; the old
French Taps remains in our Tattoo. (Wonder what Lafayette
would say?)

Taps was apparently first used in connection with military
funerals during the same campaign. Some sources say A Battery
of the Second Artillery was the first to make this use of the call;
other sources say it was B Battery of the same outfit.

Moss [31] gives this account: "During the Peninsular Campaign in
1862 a soldier of Tidball's Battery—'A' of the 2nd Artillery—was
buried at a time when the battery occupied an advanced position,
concealed in the woods. It was unsafe to fire the customary three
volleys over the grave, on account of the proximity of the enemy,
and it occurred to Captain Tidball that the sounding of Taps would
be the most appropriate ceremony that could be substituted. The
custom, thus originated, was taken up throughout the Army of the
Potomac, and finally confirmed by orders."

Colby [32] states that it was B Battery of the Third Artillery that
first used Taps at a military funeral.

[31] Colonel James A. Moss, *Officers' Manual* (Menasha, Wisconsin: George
Banta Publishing Company). First published about 1913, this book was the
bible of officers for approximately thirty years. It is still in print.

[32] Elbridge Colby, *Army Talk* (Princeton, 1942), p. 208.

The following words have been written for Taps:

> Fades the light,
> And afar
> Goeth day
> Cometh night;
> And a star
> Leadeth all,
> Speedeth all
> To their rest.

### The "Sound Off" at Parades

At parade, on the adjutant's command, "Sound Off," the band plays three chords before it starts a march and "troops the line." When the band has returned to its place and finished playing the march it repeats these three chords. They are known as the "Three Cheers."

According to Moss [33] this custom can be traced back to the time of the Crusades. Soldiers selected to go on the Crusades would form on the right of the line of troops. They were honored by having the band march and countermarch in front of their small, select group only. The three chords still sounded by the band are symbolic of the three cheers of the assembled populace during this part of the ceremony.

### Drums and "Drumhead Justice"

As we have seen, drums are probably the oldest form of musical instrument. Originally they were used in armies for the calls and signals later sounded by bugles.

They got to be quite elaborate and were accorded the same reverence as the "colors." Victories were expressed in terms of the number of enemy drums captured, just as in the case of colors.

In Marlborough's time, each unit had three different sets of drums. "Company drums" and the larger "battle drums" were simple, utilitarian things. The command or headquarters drums, however, were highly elaborate and bore the royal coat of arms.

[33] *Origin and Significance of Military Customs,* by Major James A. Moss (Menasha, Wisconsin: George Banta Publishing Company, 1917).

"Drumhead courts-martial" were instituted by Marlborough at a time when an increase in disciplinary problems required some provision for meting out prompt and "summary" justice on the battlefield. The drum, with its royal seal, was used to symbolize the royal prerogative of awarding the death sentence.

A true "drumhead trial" proceeded as follows. The headquarters drum was placed so that the royal coat of arms faced the accused. The unit commander held "summary court." Then, placing his right hand on the drum, he delivered the sentence. The drum was then turned around to signify that the power of the court was ended. "In effect this meant that the court had no power to entertain an appeal against the sentence, which was usually executed forthwith." [34]

### Cadence Marching

Primitive armies "marched" in a column-of-bunches formation without any attempt at keeping in step with each other. When tactical formations such as the phalanx were developed, it became necessary for men to keep step. But the idea of keeping step during road marches was a Roman innovation. As we saw in the section on military music, the drum was used to beat time. Galley slaves were kept in cadence by the same method.

The advantage of marching in step is something that every modern recruit has to learn for himself. In fact, "route step" is the term old soldiers apply to recruit outfits that have not yet learned this ancient lesson.

There is something about the regular rhythm of cadence marching that moves tired troops along with a little more spirit and efficiency—particularly if the step is set by music. (Ours is not a "singing army," and we have yet to develop any really popular marching songs.)

The American Army now parades at a brisk cadence of 120 steps per minute. In the old days the cadence was about thirty per cent slower, since the lesser pace was required for keeping battle formations. The French Foreign Legion still parades at a stately seventy-eight steps per minute.

The slow march of modern military funerals (approximately

[34] C. C. Soden, "Defaulters," in *Australian Army Journal*, August, 1955.

sixty steps per minute) is, of course, dictated by the solemn music prescribed for the funeral march. The "slow march," however, arose from the practice of using a heavy artillery wagon to transport the remains to the grave. This custom arose during the reign of Henry VIII. Drummers marched behind the wagon and beat what was then known as the "Dede Sounde."

### Position of Honor

Running through our customs and courtesies of the service—social as well as official—is the principle that the right side of a person or thing is the position of honor.

"The Right of the Line" was the critical side in ancient battle formations and is the place of honor in ceremonies today. The motto of the Fourteenth Infantry, "The Right of the Line," comes from the honored station General Meade directed the regiment to take in a review just after the Civil War.

The starboard (right) side of a ship is normally reserved for officers to board, while enlisted visitors and crewmen use the port gangway.

In walking with a senior or riding in a vehicle the junior is on the left. The national flag is carried or displayed on the right of all others. The right is the point of honor in heraldry.[35]

This practice probably originates from the days when gentlemen carried swords for protection. The stronger swordsman was given the position of honor (the right) so that his sword arm would be unhampered for a fast draw.

The fact that men's clothing buttons to the right and women's to the left has also been traced back to the days before pockets when people put their hands, Napoleon-like, into their coat fronts for warmth. With her "protector" on the right, a lady's coat buttoned to the left so that both she and the gentleman could slip their free hands into their coat fronts.

The American flag is properly displayed with the "field" (stars)

---

[35] Some astute student of heraldry discovered a horrifying thing a few years ago. The eagle on the officer's cap insignia was facing to the *left!* This, in the code of heraldry, symbolized cowardice. The badge makers corrected their "sinister" error in subsequent models and "dexterously" faced the bird in the proper direction.

to the flag's right. One exception is when the flag is placed over a casket, in which instance the point of honor is to the left of the body. In this case it was evidently reasoned that it was more fitting for the field to be over the heart.

### Why Medals Are Worn on the Left

One fortuitous feature of the human anatomy is that by carrying a shield on the left arm, leaving the right hand free for a weapon, the heart is afforded maximum protection by the shield. (Ancient "southpaws" did the best they could.) Considerations of protection as well as propinquity led the Crusaders to wear their small decorative crosses over the heart. This may well be why military decorations (a recent innovation) are worn on the left. How about the Russians? Well, aside from not having much affection for Christian conventions, they get so many medals that they have to hang them anywhere they can find an empty place.

### Origin of the Hand Salute

It is not possible to give the precise origin of the hand salute. From earliest times and in many races the right (weapon) hand has been raised as a greeting of friendship. The idea may have been to show that you weren't ready to use a rock or other, more civilized, weapon. Courtesy required that the inferior make the gesture first. Certainly there is some connection between this old gesture and our present salute.

Many romantic "origins" have been invented: for example, that it symbolizes the knight's gesture of raising his visor to reveal his identity as a courtesy on the approach of a superior. Another pretty myth is that the salute symbolizes a knight's shielding his eyes from the dazzling beauty of some high-born lady sitting in the bleachers of the tournament. (Why not say it symbolizes a frightened subordinate's throwing up a hand to keep from being backhanded across the jaw by a passing superior?)

The military salute has had many forms. At one time it was rendered with both hands! In old prints one may see left-handed salutes. In some instances the salute was rendered by lowering the saber with one hand and touching the cap visor with the other.

The hand salute—how it evolved.

The following explanation of the origin of the hand salute strikes me as being the most plausible. It was a long-established military custom for juniors to remove their headgear in the presence of superiors. In the British Army as late as the American Revolution a soldier saluted by removing his hat. With the advent of cumbersome headgear like the shako, busby and the bearskin which could not be readily doffed, the act of removing the hat degenerated into a gesture of grasping the visor. It finally became conventionalized into something resembling our modern hand salute.

This theory is substantiated by an entry in the order book of the Coldstream Guards, dated 3 September 1745: "The men ordered not to pull off their hats when they pass an officer, or to speak to them, but only to clap up their hands to their hats and bow as they pass." [36]

### Other Forms of Salute

The idea of holding your weapon in a harmless position appears to be a universal and a very old way of showing respect. Tomes mentions that even the Arab of the Sahara salutes by trailing the point of his spear on the ground.

The movement of "Present arms" with the rifle—in which the piece is held vertically in front of the body, trigger and sling forward —is a token of submitting your weapon to the person being honored. The origin of this movement has been traced to the return of Charles II to England in 1660 to claim the throne. Colonel Monk's Coldstream Regiment, which professed the desire to place themselves at his service, was formed in a field. When the monarch approached, the command was given to "Present your weapons for service under His Majesty." Each man held his pike or musket forward in the position we now call "high port." Then, "Ground your weapons" was ordered. The next command was, "In His Majesty's cause, recover your weapons."

The King, with an eye for the dramatic, ordered that this ceremony be prescribed as the "Present Arms" for all future inspections as a mark of respect.[37]

[36] Quoted in *Old Times Under Arms,* by Colonel Cyril Field (London, 1939).

[37] Soden, C. C., "How It Began," *Australian Army Journal,* April, 1955.

## Sword Salute

The first movement of the sword salute—bringing the hilt up opposite the chin, point of the sword in the air—is said to be a relic of the days when the Crusader kissed the cross (hilt) before battle. The second motion—lowering the point to the ground—symbolizes the trust of "putting down your guard."

## Gun Salutes

High military and civil officials are honored by a prescribed number of gun blasts. This custom has been traced to the days when it took a long time to reload guns. By firing off all your guns at the approach of a Very Important Person (V.I.P.), you rendered your ship, fort or battery defenseless.

Through the years there evolved a prescribed number of guns to be fired for various V.I.P.'s (in accordance with the importance of their positions). Why are salutes fired in odd numbers? Apparently this is an old naval superstition which has been preserved through the years.

## Dipping the Flag in Salute

Ships used to dip their sails as a sign of respect. In so doing they reduced their speed and allowed themselves to be overhauled. This is now symbolized by dipping the ensign (the flag, that is, not the officer).

The American Army never dips the national color ("Stars and Stripes") in salute. Other colors, such as regimental colors, are dipped in salute to the unit commander or higher ranking officer as they pass the reviewing stand. The only other time the organizational color or standard is dipped is to honor the national anthem or "To the Color."

Flying the flag at half-staff ("half-*mast*" in the Navy) probably comes from the naval custom of lowering sails in salute or as a sign of distress.

## Inspecting the Guard of Honor

Now a mere courtesy, the escort or guard of honor once served a real purpose.[38] It is customary for a V.I.P. to "inspect" the guard

[38] The "guard of honor" and the "escort of honor" are terms used in our Army Regulations and Field Manuals as being one and the same thing.

of honor. In this case he is not looking for rusty weapons, but is returning the guard's courtesy by taking a close look at the fine military appearance of these select troops. A real general does more than pass hurriedly along the ranks of the guard of honor. He usually looks each man in the face and stops from time to time to chat with one of the soldiers or compliment him on his appearance.

Now, this last custom is a vestige of a very real "inspection" that was held three centuries ago. Here is the story. When Charles II came back from exile in 1660 to claim the throne of England, a crack cavalry regiment, formerly with the late Cromwell, decided to offer its allegiance to the king. A squadron was sent from the regiment to meet the king. Outriders from the royal party met the cavalry on a desolate stretch of the country and reported back to the king. With some justifiable suspicion, the latter went forward on foot with a lone attendant to assure himself that this was not a trap. Charles passed slowly along the ranks of the troopers, who had drawn up alongside the road, and carefully scrutinized each man's face for signs of treachery. Convinced of the sincerity of the offer, Charles then accepted the allegiance of the commander and ordered the squadron to escort him on to London. (This outfit is now the Royal Horse Guards.)

A short time later, Colonel Monk's Coldstream Regiment marched down from Scotland and asked permission to enter the King's service. Charles had the regiment formed and inspected them as he had the cavalrymen. He then accepted them as the "Coldstream Guards." [39]

### Precedence of Troops at Parades and Reviews

The slowest moving branch normally has the "honor" of being placed on the "right of the line" during ceremonies (except funerals). At the discretion of the commander of troops this can be varied. However, this general rule avoids a squabble and, since units normally "dress" to the right when marching, it assures that the infantry does not get left behind.

Precedence among military units—very much as among people—

---

[39] The "Present Arms" form of salute was originated at this same formation. See page 47.

is normally determined by age. This is sort of a cowardly solution, but it lessens the chances of hurt feelings.

The Coldstream Guards were originally designated by Charles II (1660) as the senior regiment of the British service (because they were the first to come over to his cause in the Restoration). This entitled them to the position of "right of the line" at ceremonies. When Charles later created his Grenadier Guards, he was so proud of them (being his own idea) that he arbitrarily designated them the senior British regiment. He smoothed the feathers of the Coldstream Guards by specially authorizing them to occupy the extreme left position of the line. (Possibly this was on the recommendation of an alert "Provost," to minimize the chances of a fight during ceremonies.)

The head of the table has long been the position of honor, with succeedingly "honorable" positions going from the right and left down to the foot. How would you handle the problem of seating a group of important people whom you wanted to treat as equals? King Arthur's boys solved the problem by making their table round.[40]

But let's get back to the present-day American Army.

In parades and ceremonies in which Army, Navy and Air Force troops participate, regulations prescribe that West Point Cadets will lead. Next in column come the Midshipmen of Annapolis and the Cadets of the Coast Guard Academy. Succeeding positions for U. S. troops are: 4. Army; 5. Marine Corps; 6. Navy; 7. Air Force; 8. Coast Guard; 9. National Guard; 10. Organized Reserve Corps; 11. Marine Corps Reserve; 12. Naval Reserve; 13. Air Force National Guard; 14. Air Force Reserve; 15. Coast Guard Reserve; 16. Other Reserve training organizations of the Army, the Marine Corps, the Navy, the Air Force, and the Coast Guard, in that order, respectively.[41]

---

[40] Medieval history has several examples of "Knights of the Round Table" who organized themselves into sort of an early-day Ku Klux Klan and took "justice" into their own hands. One such table is preserved. It has thirteen places, the unlucky one labeled and left vacant for "Judas." The term "round table" was also applied to a type of tourney.

[41] US Army, SR 600–25–1, Par. 6.

# CHAPTER 3

# Origin of Military Words

THIS chapter consists of a list of about a hundred common military words and their origins. Normally you would expect to find such material relegated in small print to an appendix. I think, however, a quick look will convince you that in the derivations of these words we have a rather complete outline of military origins.[1] Many of the terms have been mentioned elsewhere in the book; they are repeated here for convenience of reference.

**adjutant**  From a Latin word meaning "to assist." Hence an officer who assists the commander. The office was introduced into the English Army in 1660 (Foster).

**Amazon**  While this word is of little military importance, it has an interesting derivation. *Amazon* is Greek for "without breast." According to legend these mythological women warriors burned off their right breasts as children so that they could shoot the bow more effectively.

**ambulance**  From the French *hôpital ambulant,* "moving hospital." Originally a temporary field hospital, the word now means a vehicle used for moving wounded.

**ambush**  Formerly "embush," it can be traced back to the Old French *embucher* ("to go into the woods") and the Italian *emboscata* ("hidden in the woods"). Webster points out that *"ambuscade* is now the regular military term for the legitimate disposition of troops in concealment; *ambush* is less formal and is often applied to such lying in wait as is unfair or cowardly."

---

[1] Sources and authorities are listed at the end of this chapter.

**ammunition**   Latin, *munitio,* meaning generally "fortify by building a wall." The word "munitions" came to mean any provisions for defense. The "a" got added in English by mistake: the French *la munition* was erroneously assumed to have been *l'ammunition.* Both words, "ammunition" and "munitions," are now used in English as being roughly synonymous; "munitions" is, however, generally more inclusive.

**army**   In French, *armée,* which in turn is from the Latin *armare,* "to arm." Armada is what the word-wizards call a "doublet": it comes from the same origin as "army" but in taking another route has acquired a different meaning ("a fleet of warships").

**arsenal**   Possibly from the Latin *arx navalis,* "naval citadel"; but more likely from the Arabic *dar al sina 'ah,* "a court or house of industry or manufacture." (Webster)

**artillery**   French, *artiller,* "to equip." The word originally referred to all engines of war and military equipment. By the sixteenth century the word began to mean "guns"; by the eighteenth century it began to refer also to the service that handled the guns. (Foster) (See page 13).

**barrage**   In French, *tir de barrage,* literally "a type of fire which 'bars' or obstructs [the enemy]." See "barricade," below.

**barrel**   The use of this word to mean a part of a rifle or cannon does not come from its resemblance to the receptacle we ordinarily think of as a barrel. Rather, both words come from the same source: "something made of bars." An early type of cannon was constructed by welding long wrought-iron bars together and shrinking iron hoops around them. The construction method was abandoned, but the term remained.

**barricade**   There is a picturesque theory that this military term comes from the Italian *barrica* ("barrel"), and originally meant "made of barrels"—of which barricades for street fighting might logically consist. It is more plausible, however, to believe that the word "bar" is at the root of both "barrel" (made of bars) and "barricade" (a thing that "bars" the enemy's advance).

**batman**   (British term for an officer's "orderly"—which see). *Bât* is Old French for "burden." The batman (or batboy) was the soldier who used to take care of the officers' equipment carried on the "bat [pack] horses." When the term "bathorse" disappeared, the word "batman" remained for an officer's orderly.

**battalion** From the Italian *battaglione,* "little battle." Let's say that an organization large enough to "fight a little battle" became known as a battalion. That is not a very scientific derivation, but is pretty close.

**battery** From the Latin *battere,* "to beat." The gun battery is so called because it "beats on" the enemy. "Battle" and "battalion" both go back to this same root.

**bayonet** Probably from Bayonne, France, where they are alleged to have been first made. This convenient "origin" has never been proved, but neither has any other.

**"Beefeaters"** (Yeomen of the Guard) An "eater" in medieval England was a servant. Presumably this term originated from the fact that he got his "board" as well as his "bed." A "loaf eater" was the lowest form of servant. The soldier, being the highest class of servant, got the preferred chow: beef. (Radford) The venerable (1802) James says that these people were originally called "Buffetiers" because they were "stationed by the sideboard at great royal dinners." See also page 23.

**berserk** This is an honorable warrior word that journalists often confuse with "amuck" (or *amok*)." *Berserk* (Old Norse for "bearskin") was a Scandinavian warrior who performed feats of superhuman skill, strength and valor in battle—sort of a "one-man army." To go "berserk" means, therefore, to perform valorously in battle. *Amok,* on the other hand, is Malay for "furious" (*amoq*). It means a murderous frenzy. Charge through Times Square at high noon indiscriminately killing people, and you are "running amuck" —you have not "gone berserk." The Moro *juramentado,* which our troops encountered in the Philippines around the turn of the century, was a cross between the berserker and the man who had run amuck. Moro warriors would work themselves up into a religious frenzy, take dope, wrap strands of wet bamboo at intervals up their arms and legs (to cause maddening pain, and also serve as tourniquets if they were wounded). Then they would take off and see how many Christians they could kill before expiring themselves. Our .45-caliber pistol—with its great impact—was developed to stop them. The *juramentado,* like the World War II Japanese *kamikaze* ("divine wind") was on a suicide mission. The *berserker,* on the other hand, was interested in staying alive if possible.

**billet**    French *billet de logement,* a "ticket for lodgings." Soldiers have not been furnished barracks until fairly recent years. They were "billeted" on the populace.

**bivouac**    German *bewachen,* "to watch." The term was originally applied to a small outpost that was sent out from the main body of troops to keep watch while the others rested in camp. Later, "bivouac" came to be applied to the camp itself rather than just the outpost.

**bomb**    Latin, *bombus,* "a noise," from Greek *bombos,* "a deep hollow sound" (Webster). The word originally applied to cannon balls. (The first aerial bombs were dropped from unmanned balloons on Venice by the Austrians in 1849.)

**"Boots and Saddle"**    An old Cavalry command to mount. As a matter of interest, it comes from the French *boute selle,* meaning "put on the saddle." It has nothing to do with boots. (Radford)

**brevet**    An Old French word from the Latin *brevis,* "brief." As far back as 1600 a brevet was described by Cotgrave as a short note giving an officer temporary elevation in authority. (Harrison) See page 92.

**brigade**    This is a sixteenth-century French word which corresponds to the Spanish *brigar,* "to brawl," and the Italian *brigare,* "to fight." Like the word "battalion," it came to be applied to a body of contesting troops of a more or less arbitrarily agreed-on size.

**brigand**    This word ties in closely with "brigade." A "brigand" was originally a lightly armored, irregular foot soldier. It got to mean "bandit" from the fact that many mercenary outfits turned into outlaws when the war ended and they faced unemployment.

**bugle**    Short for *"bugle horn." Bugle* is an obsolete term for the bison or ox, from whose horns the musical ancestor of the instrument now known as a bugle was first made.

**bulldozer**   (See Chapter 5.)

**cadre**   From the French *cadre,* "a frame." A military cadre is a small group of key officers and noncoms around which a new unit can be formed by shipping in recruits.

**caliber**   From the Latin *con libra,* "of equal weight." It is now a linear measure of the inside diameter of a weapon's bore.

**camp**   Latin, *campus,* "field." A camp is a military installation "in the field."

**canteen**   Italian *cantina,* "wine cellar." The word was first used in the military profession for the place where soldiers got refreshments on a military reservation. Then it was applied to the flask which soldiers carried on a march. Through World War I the use of "canteen" in the first sense was common. (A squad leader, when asked to account for three absentees, is alleged to have reported: "One's in the canteen, one's in the latrine, and one I ain't never done seen.") This fine old soldier word has fallen victim to modernization; the Post Exchange (PX) has taken its place.

**cantonment**   The Latin *cantone,* "corner," gave the French *cantonner,* meaning "to distribute troops into cantons or districts." (A "canton" is one of the states in the Swiss confederation and in heraldry is a rectangular division of a shield.)

**captain**   From the Latin *caput,* "head." Although the Captain could be the head of any organization, by convention the rank has long been associated with the officer commanding a company-size unit (100 to 200 men).

**"carpet knight"**   The early knights earned and were awarded their spurs on the battlefield. When the administrative type began to appear as a necessary member of the military hierarchy, certain noncombatants earned and were awarded their golden spurs of knighthood on the carpet of the sovereign's palace. They were dubbed "carpet knights."

**cavalry**   From the Latin *caballus* (horse) came the word "cavalier," thence "cavalry."

**chevron**   French *chevron,* "rafter" (see page 27).

**colonel**   Probably from the Italian *colonello,* "a little column" (technically, it should be *colonella*). See page 9.

**colors**   The term arose in the early seventeenth century when units started carrying flags which represented a great variety of hues. (See page 32.)

**commando**   A Portuguese word adopted by the Boers and then by the British. Originally it meant simply "a military force [command]." In South Africa it came to be applied to an expedition or raid.

**communications**   First used by military writers in the nineteenth century. It comes from the Latin *communicatus,* "made common." In this sense, it is "knowledge" that is "made common" between people who "communicate."

**company**   The Latin *cum* (with) and *pane* (bread) meant "messmates."

**comrade**   From the Spanish *camerad-o,* which came in turn from the Latin *camera,* "room." It originally meant "roommate."

**condottieri**   (Italian mercenaries)   From the Latin *conductitii,* "led men." While the word was originally restricted to the leader, it came to mean his men. The word was applied to such famous non-Italian mercenary leaders as Sir John Hawkwood, Tilly and Wallenstein.

**corporal**   From the Italian *capo di squadra,* "squad [square] leader."

**defile**   From the French *fil,* a "string." Hence a narrow place through which soldiers had to pass in file.

**doughboy**   (see Chapter 5).

**dragoons**   (mounted infantry)   The muzzles of early muskets were made with ornamental dragons' heads as an allusion to this fanciful animal's characteristic of breathing fire. Since mounted infantry were armed with short-barreled muskets ("dragoons"), they became known as Dragoons.

**drill**   From the seventeenth-century Dutch *drillen,* "to turn."

**drum**   Teutonic *trom,* "drum."

**dud** (a shell that fails to explode) Possibly from the Dutch *dood,* "dead." (Radford).

**dumdum** (an expanding bullet) The name comes from the town of Dumdum, near Calcutta, India. Webster says they were first *made* there; Shipley says they were first *used* there by the British Bengal Artillery.

**echelon** A French word meaning "step of a ladder."

**enfilade** From the French *enfiler,* "to thread."

**engineer** One who deals with "engines" (of war). See page 13.

**fatigue** In the military sense, "fatigue" (or "fatigue duty") is the work soldiers do which is not connected with purely martial exploits (e.g., cleaning up their barracks, digging garbage pits, etc.). The word "fatigue" was once used in common English to signify "toil" or "labor." So the military term "fatigue" is probably of literal origin and applies to the tiresome tasks of military housekeeping. "Fatigue clothes" are the uniforms prescribed for work details.

**fife** Old German *pfifa,* "pipe."

**file** A number of men in depth. From French *fil,* "thread." (Men side by side are a "rank.")

**furlough** Dutch *verlof,* "leave of absence."

**garrison** Old French *guerir,* "to preserve." Presumably a garrison is put in a place to "preserve" it from enemy capture. In current usage the word implies an administrative rather than a tactical role.

**general officer** The officer in general command of all troops.

**grenade** A weapon invented in 1594 and given the Spanish name for pomegranate (which, in turn, means "the fruit full of seeds").

**Guards** Elite troops who "guarded" the King.

**guerrilla** A diminutive of the Spanish *guerra* (war). The word first meant "little war." Later it was applied to the irregular troops who waged the "little war." The term originated during Napoleon's Spanish campaign.

**havoc**    From the Old French *havot*, "plunder." Originally, when one of the contesting bodies of troops raised the cry of "Havoc!" it meant they considered the battle won and the troops were authorized to start plundering. Later the expression seems to have had a larger meaning; the side that raised the cry of "Havoc!" was announcing that no quarter would be given or expected (i.e., no prisoners). This led to such excesses of battlefield slaughter that efforts were made to abolish the practice. William the Conqueror is said to have forbidden the crying of havoc by his troops.

**helmet**    Anglo-Saxon *helm*, from Teutonic root *hal* or *kal*, "to cover." A helmet is a "little helm."

**howitzer**    Czech word from the Hussites of Jan Žižka (fifteenth century). It is related to the German *haufnice*, a "sling."

**hussars**    Hungarian *huszar*, from *husz*, "twenty." Every twentieth man in the country was drafted for service in the Light Cavalry on the Turkish frontier.

**infantry**    The consensus is that this word for foot soldiers actually comes from "infant," although there has been much straining to find a more noble origin. The French *infanterie* (from which our word comes) is from the Italian *infanteria*, which comes from *infante*, meaning child, servant and foot soldier. "Infant" is from the Latin *in* (not) and *fari* (to speak). Until a person was big enough to speak he was an infant. The connection between infantry and child or servant has a connotation of inferiority which is no accident. At the time "infant" was linked with "foot soldiers," the cavalry was the senior or elite service. When the infantryman again began to dominate the battlefield (as he had in the days of Rome and as he does today) the Spanish foot soldier led the way. This is probably why "infantry" has been connected with the Spanish title *infante*. Some writers have assumed that infantry was the elite force commanded by the *Infante*, or Spanish crown prince. However, the Spanish (and Portuguese) *infante* was any legitimate son of the king; the eldest son was known as the *Principe*. (Webster) There is a far-fetched but prevalent theory that foot troops are called infantry because early generals affectionately referred to them as "my boys."

**"iron rations"**  So called because they were carried in a tin, airtight box. (Radford)

**Janissary** or **Janizary** (elite Turkish infantry existing from the fourteenth to the nineteenth century)  Turkish *yeni* (new) and *cheri* (troops). Janissaries were originally the personal slaves of the Sultan. Later, they were elite troops made up of Christians who had been captured while very young and subjected to a strict system of training. The organization was abolished after 1826 when the Janissaries revolted and tried to seize control of the government.

**jeep**  (see Chapter 5).

**jingoes** (people who advocate war)  A name given to the war party in Great Britain which wanted the British to get into the Russo–Turkish War of 1877–78. The term came from the song: "We don't want to fight, but, by jingo, if we do, We've got the ships, we've got the men, we've got the money too." (Radford)

**khaki**  Indian *khaki,* "dust colored." See page 28 for origin of material.

**lieutenant**  French *lieu* (place) *tenant* (holding). He is the officer who "holds the place of" another. By usage, it has come to mean the officer who holds the place of a captain.

**logistics**  Originally the duties of the Quartermaster were known as "logistics," since this officer was concerned with *logis* or "quarters" for the troops. For many years the Quartermaster General was the principal staff officer and the word "logistics" was used to designate all staff work. See page 16.

**magazine**  Arabic *makhzan,* "storehouses." It was originally used in our language to mean a military storehouse for weapons and ammunition. The use of the word in the literary sense originated in 1731 with publication of *The Gentleman's Magazine,* which advertised itself as "A monthly collection to treasure up as in a magazine, the most remarkable pieces on the subjects above-mentioned." (The word "pieces" is also being played on; weapons in a military magazine were then known as "pieces," as they still are today.) (Radford)

**Major** Originally "Sergeant Major" (see page 8). "Major" means simply "greater"; the Sergeant Major was the "greater sergeant." The political title of mayor comes from the fact that this man occupies an office "greater than" that of the other city officials. (Harrison)

**Major General** Originally Sergeant-Major General. See page 8.

**maneuver** or **manoeuvre** Latin *manuum* (manual) and *opera* (labor).

**Marshal** Old High German *mara schalh,* "horse servant." The interesting thing about the "Marshal" is that he started as a very menial servant and is today the highest officer in many foreign armies. The term "Field Marshal" was developed to distinguish the military from the civilian marshal. The word "constable," incidentally, is from the same horsy origin as marshal: the Late Latin *comes stabuli,* "stable attendant."

**martinet** This is the term for a strict military disciplinarian. A Colonel (later General) Martinet in the armies of Louis XIV was famous for the strict discipline of his Model Regiment (formed in 1668). Brown, however, quotes a mid-nineteenth-century British authority (W. L. Blackley) as stating that the Swiss have an evil spirit in their ancient superstitions called "martinet." This would indicate that the term may have been introduced into the military lexicon by Swiss mercenaries. Shipley points out that the French do not use "martinet" in the same sense as we do. He also points out that the word existed in Old French as the word for a cat-o'-nine-tails. Possibly the French general adopted "Martinet" as a *nom de guerre* when he was promoted to Inspector General of Infantry.

**mercenary** From Latin *merces,* "wages," "reward." Originally the term was applied to anybody who worked solely for pay or some other reward. Now it applies (in the military sense) only to soldiers who hire themselves out to fight for another country.

**mess** Probably from Latin *mensa,* a "table"; or a form of the verb *mittere,* "to put or place" (on a table, for example). *Mess* originally meant "an amount of meat served to four people." The French still use the word in this sense, but they also use *mess* in the same military sense as we do.

**mortar**  So called because of its resemblance to the druggist's mortar. The first military mortars probably were pits bored into rock.

**mufti**  English officers were represented in a number of early-nineteenth-century plays as wearing tasseled caps and dressing gowns while off duty. Somebody suggested that they resembled the Mohammedan officials known as *mufti*. The word was adopted in the Indian Army for any civilian clothes worn by officers when off duty. (Shipley) The American press has found this a convenient antonym for "uniform" but it is little used by soldiers (who prefer "civvies" or "cits").

**orderly**  In England an "orderly" is a person responsible for neatness and cleanliness. We use the word in this sense for hospital, mess, day-room and other types of orderly. (See page 146 for discussion of officers' orderlies.) In a related but different sense, "orderly" has to do with orders. An "Orderly Officer" (or noncommissioned officer) was formerly used to deliver orders. An "orderly book" was one in which orders were recorded. (See also "dog robber" and "striker," in Chapter 5.)

**ordnance**  In the fifteenth century an ordinance (with an *i*) was promulgated to standardize the size and caliber of guns. Somehow the *i* got dropped out of the word used to designate the weapons themselves. The Master-General of Ordnance (without an *i*) was an office created as early as 1414. (Foster)

**pack**  Twelfth-century Flemish for "pack horse." (See also "batman.")

**parade**  Spanish *parada*, from *parar*, "to prepare." The word was picked up in 1625 by the English Army when they were fighting the Spanish in the Netherlands. "Parading" a guard originally meant preparing it for duty.

**patrol**  French *patrouille* from Old French *patoueil*, "mud." It means "to paddle in mud."

**pawn**  Now the least important piece in chess, a pawn was originally a foot soldier. It was corrupted from the Latin *pedanus,* literally "foot slogger." The Spanish *peon* (serf) and the word "pedestrian" come from the same root.

**pistol**  French and Greek *pistole,* "pipe." The Czech *pistal* also means "pipe." The weapon was first used around 1540, when it was nothing more than a pipe on the end of a stick. This weakens the more picturesque theory that the word comes from Pistoia, Italy, where (Foster says) pistols were first made in the early sixteenth century.

**platoon**  Latin *pila,* "ball," which evolved into the French *pelote,* "small bundle." A platoon, then, was a "small bundle" or group of soldiers.

**ponton**  This is the military spelling (and pronunciation) for "pontoon," a boat or other float on which a floating bridge is built. The military form of the word is probably due to its derivation from the French Army in which the word is *ponton.*

**Private**  Used from the sixteenth century in the sense of a "private man," rather than an "officer" or office holder. The term came into use after the abolishment of the feudal system and signified that the individual now had the privilege of making a private contract of military service, rather than being forced to serve a feudal master.

**Quartermaster**  The man in charge of providing "quarters" for troops. The office dates from the *Reiter* organization of the fifteenth century. See page 16.

**rank** (a number of men side by side)  Old German *hrang,* a "ring," and later a "row" of men. See also "file." The expression "rank and file," therefore, means the soldiers composing the ranks and files of a military formation. It does not mean the officers ("people *with* rank") and the "files" (soldier slang for "individuals").

**recruit**  In Latin, *recrescere,* "to grow again." Recruits, then, are new men to replace losses and permit the unit to "grow again" to its original size and effectiveness.

**regiment** In Latin, *regiment*, "rule" (in the sense of "regulation"). The term was applied to a military organization that was under the rule of a colonel.

**retreat** In Latin, *retrahere*, "to withdraw." Tactically, this word means to withdraw from enemy contact. But the ceremony of Retreat and the bugle call "Retreat" signify a retirement from the day's administrative activities, not the enemy's tactical endeavors. To "beat retreat" in the old days did not mean to "bug out" or to "how able" (see Chapter 5). Before the use of bugles to sound calls, drums were used.

**reveille** French *reveillez -vous*, "Wake up!"

**Sam Browne belt** According to Ffoulkes, this type of belt was invented by Sir Basil Montgomery in 1878 and worn by General Sir Sam Browne in 1879. Sir James Douglas devised a similar belt and improvements were made in 1885. The British Army adopted the belt officially on April 24, 1900.

**sentinel** According to Shipley, this word is of naval origin; *sentina* (Latin) was an outhouse and also the hold of a ship where the bilge collected. A "sentinel" was posted to sound the alarm when it was time to man the pumps. Webster traces the word back to the Latin *sentire*, "to perceive by the senses." Although Webster's definition is more sensible, Shipley's, it must be admitted, holds considerable water. It has also been suggested, in all seriousness, that the army sentinel was so named from the resemblance between a sentry box and a latrine (outhouse). Certainly this latter theory will find many supporters among the rank and file of the Army who have formed their own unprintable opinion about guard duty.

**sentry** Probably from the same source as "sentinel," rather than from the French *sentier* (path—around which a guard would walk). Fortescue suggests that the word was corrupted from "centinel." The latter word is from "century," the term applied to the 100-man Roman companies. Until the beginning of the eighteenth century the private soldier in England was known as a "private centinel."

**sergeant** Latin *servire*, "to serve." Originally used in law, a *serviens* during the days of chivalry was also a military servant.

**sharpshooter**  Probably from German *scharffschutze,* which has the same meaning. The term does not come from the Sharp's Rifle, patented in 1852. "Sharpshooter" units are listed as early as 1805 in the British Army. Two regiments of U. S. Sharpshooters were raised during the Civil War. The term is now used in the U. S. Army to designate a qualification in marksmanship which is between Expert (the highest) and Marksman (the lowest).

**shrapnel**  Invented by General Shrapnel of the British Army in the early nineteenth century. See page 149 for comments on usage.

**slogan**  Gaelic *slaugh* (host) and *ghairm* (outcry). Originally a battle cry of the old Highland clans, a slogan is now something used to sell soap or politicians.

**soldier**  Latin *solidus,* a coin with which soldiers were paid.

**squad**  French *escouade;* Italian *squadra,* a square or four men.

**squadron**  "A large square."

**staff**  The officers who assist the commander may be called a staff because they are "leaned on" for advice (Foster). Or the term may be derived from the fact that these officers used to carry a staff (stick) as a symbol of their office. (A vestige of this "staff" as a symbol of authority—like the king's mace—may be seen in the Field Marshal's baton.) (Fortescue)

**strafe**  German *strafen,* "to punish." The World War I German war cry *Gott strafe England* meant "God punish [not strafe] England." (We now use the word in English to mean "machine-gun ground targets from low-flying aircraft.")

**strategy**  Greek *strategos,* "a general." The art of the general.

**tactics**  Greek *taktike,* "to arrange." The art of arranging troops on the battlefield. The military mind has been straining since the battle of Marathon for a clear-cut distinction between "strategy" and "tactics." For practical purposes, strategy is the movement of troops *to* the battlefield; tactics is the maneuvering of troops *on* the battlefield.

**tank**  When the British secretly moved their experimental armored vehicles up to the front during World War I to try them against the Germans they were covered with tarpaulins and labeled "tanks" (i.e., cisterns). After they ceased to be a "secret weapon," the name "tanks" was retained for lack of a more convenient one.

**tattoo** Dutch tap (tap or faucet) and *toe* (off). See page 40.

**troop** French *troupe;* German *treiben,* "a flock or drove." Possibly connected with Latin *turba,* "a crowd."

**vanguard** or **van** French *avant-garde,* "advance guard."

**wagon** Dutch *waggon.*

**war** Teutonic *werre.*

### SOURCES, AUTHORITIES AND ACKNOWLEDGMENTS

*Organization: How Armies Are Formed for War,* by Colonel Hubert Foster (London: Hugh Rees, 1913), is the book to which I am principally indebted for the concept of this chapter as well as for much of the material in it.

Sir John W. Fortescue, mentioned throughout this book, has been another prime source. See main bibliography (page 172) for works of his consulted.

Other authors mentioned in the chapter are:

Brown, Ivor, *I Give You My Word* and *Say the Word* (1 volume) (New York, E. P. Dutton, 1948).

Colby, Elbridge, *Army Talk* (Princeton, 1942).

Ffoulkes, Charles, *Arms and Armament* (London, 1945).

Harrison, Michael, "The Origin of British Military Ranks," in the *Territorial and Home Guard Magazine,* June, 1955.

Mathews, Mitford M. (ed.), *A Dictionary of Americanisms* (Chicago, 1951).

Radford, Edwin, *Unusual Words and How They Came About* (New York, Philosophical Library, 1946).

Shipley, Joseph T., *Dictionary of Word Origins* (New York, Philosophical Library, 1945).

Tomes, Major C. T., "Old Military Customs Still Extant," *Journal of the Royal United Services Institute* (London, 1925).

Standard works consulted were (of course):

Funk & Wagnalls' *New Standard Dictionary* (New York, 1946).

*Webster's New International Dictionary,* Second Edition, Unabridged (Springfield, Mass., 1955).

*Shorter Oxford Dictionary,* Sir James A. Murray, ed. (Oxford, 1936).

*Universal Military Dictionary* (Fourth Edition), by Charles James (London, 1816). (First published in 1802.)

CHAPTER 4

# Military Americana

### Colonial Beginnings

THE first American military leader was undoubtedly Miles Standish. In 1621 this former English soldier was unanimously elected "military captain" of the Plymouth Pilgrims who landed from the *Mayflower*.

The early colonists formed voluntary military associations for defense. These were called "bands" or "train bands"—terms which go back to the ancient Saxon Fyrd and the Posse Comitatus of feudal times. (Originally the term was "trained bands." [1])

On October 7, 1636, there were bands in Dorchester, Charlestown, Watertown, Newton, Saugus, Ipswich and Boston.[2] According to official "lineage determination," five of them were organized on this date into the North Regiment.[3] Two others, the East and Boston Regiments, were also created on this date.

### The Army's Oldest Outfits

The 182d Infantry Regiment (Fifth Massachusetts—Middlesex Regiment) and the 101st Engineer Battalion of the Massachusetts National Guard are the country's oldest military organizations of any component still in existence. They owe this distinction to an

[1] Lawson, Cecil C. P., *A History of the Uniforms of the British Army,* vol. I (London, 1940), p. 185.

[2] Whitman, Zacheriah G., *An Historical Sketch of the Ancient and Honorable Artillery Company* (Boston, 1820), p. 6.

[3] Department of the Army, *The Army Lineage Book,* vol. II: Infantry (Washington, 1953), p. 520.

unbroken lineage from the North and East Regiments, respectively, of 1636.

Boston's "Ancient and Honorable Artillery Company" is another "military organization" which dates from earliest colonial days. It should be pointed out that this venerable unit has never been a part of the Army. It is now strictly a veterans' organization. However, its history gives us a good picture of early American military organization.

Up until 1660 the wars of England had been fought by a system of *levée en masse*. The "common militia" was organized in each county and commanded by the Lord Lieutenant under the authority of the complex but effective county system of local government. Then "volunteer militia" units came into being. These were to a certain extent in competition (for men) with the "common" militia; they were organized primarily by wealthier men in the cities.

One famous "city train band" was the "Honourable Artillery Company" of London. This "artillery" company, incidentally, was originally composed of archers.

The colonists, some of whom apparently had belonged to the London City Train Band, submitted a petition in 1637 to Governor Winthrop for a charter of incorporation. They wanted to organize the scattered train bands of the colony into an organization more capable of dealing with the Indians. The "common militia" concept had already permitted formation of three regiments (see above). However, the proposed new organization of "volunteer militia" was killed by the governor in terms that have been echoed by American statesmen ever since. For this reason they are worth quoting:

Divers gentlemen and others being joined in a military company, desired to be made a corporation, but the council considering from the example of the Praetorian band among the Romans, and Templars in Europe, how dangerous it might be to erect a standing authority of military men, which might easily in time overthrow the civil power, thought fit to stop it betimes; yet they were allowed to be a company, subordinate to all authority.[4]

"The Ancient" was accordingly organized in June, 1638, and exists today with headquarters at Faneuil Hall, Boston.

[4] Whitman, *op. cit.*, p. 7.

### Earliest American Military Operations

While the American Army did not exist until 1775, our ancestors in this country did a good deal of fighting before that date. These "Colonial Wars" are important in that they did much to shape our military thinking.

Trouble with the Indians led to the organization of the Massachusetts "train bands" (above) into three regiments in 1636. Our ancestors were getting tired of dodging snipers on their way to church. So in 1637 they started a series of wars to eradicate some of their more pesky Indian neighbors. By 1655, half of the Pequot Tribe had been killed and the remainder concentrated into two villages. Another "war" ended in 1676 with the extermination of "King Philip" and 4,000 of his braves.

During the late seventeenth century, border warfare took place between French colonies in Canada and English settlements in New England and New York. Dignified with the name of King William's War, this fracas was a series of bloody raids in which neither side had any particular plan of operations and nothing decisive was accomplished.

A Massachusetts-Connecticut force under Sir William Phips captured Port Royal in 1690 and made an unsuccessful attack against Quebec. A military force from South Carolina took St. Augustine from the Spanish in 1702, but was unable to hold it. In 1745, William Pepperell led 4,000 New England colonials in an amateurish but successful assault against the formidable French fort of Louisbourg at the entrance to the Gulf of St. Lawrence.

A Major George Washington was sent by the Governor of Virginia in 1753 to demand French withdrawal from an area claimed to be "Virginia territory." Washington led 350 Virginia militia up the Monongahela Valley the next year and was defeated by 700 French troops at Fort Necessity (now Confluence, Pennsylvania). This was the start of the French and Indian War.

The first pitched battle to be fought on American soil, according to Montross,[5] was the Battle of Lake George (N. Y.) in 1756. In a determined dawn-to-dusk fight against French regulars, the Americans carried the day with a charge at sunset.

[5] Lynn Montross, *War Through the Ages* (New York: Harper, 1944).

Our American prejudice against regular troops dates from this early period. While arguing that such forces would be a threat to civil authority, the real objection was undoubtedly their expense. "So they 'economized' by spending many times what a regular force would have cost, living constantly in uneasiness and dread, risking their independence, their property and their lives." [6]

Our earliest military experiences show American militia to be just as unreliable in battle as the militia of any other nation in any other age of history. George Washington saw this lesson but was never able to communicate it to the people.

### Birth of the American Army

The Continental Army was created June 14, 1775—the Army's official birthday. On this date Congress authorized ten companies of riflemen to be raised in Virginia, Maryland and Pennsylvania. The "New England Army," which was already besieging the British in Boston, was taken over later the same year as part of the Continental Army.

Maximum strength ever attained by the Continental Army was about 35,000 men (November, 1778). The total number of troops to serve with the Continental Army during the Revolution is estimated between 250,000 and 400,000. The following casualty figures, although far from complete, are recorded: Killed, 4,044; wounded, 6,004; captured 6,642; missing, 2,124.[7]

Between 1775 and 1950 our Army participated in ninety-nine principal wars, expeditions, campaigns, occupations and other disturbances.[8] Korea brings the figure up to a round 100. Not bad for a nation that is nonmilitaristic!

### When Our Army Numbered Only Eighty Men

George Washington—to whose personal character and determination the country really owes its independence—gave up command of the Army just two days before Christmas of 1783. It is ironic that only twenty people showed up for the farewell ceremony. The year 1784 started off with some 4,000,000 Americans in

[6] Bond and Carey, *Wars of the American Nation* (Annapolis, Md., 1923).
[7] Official Adjutant-General figures.
[8] Official list of the Adjutant General, *Army Almanac*.

full possession of their independence and approximately 800,000 square miles of real estate. The Army numbered 700 rank and file —the vestige of the eighty-six-odd regiments and separate battalions of the Continental Line.

On June 2, 1784, the Continental Congress gave birth to this remarkable declaration abolishing the Army:

> And whereas, standing armies in time of peace are inconsistent with the principles of republican governments, dangerous to the liberties of a free people, and generally converted into destructive engines for establishing despotism;
>
> It is therefore resolved . . . that the commanding officer be and he is hereby directed to discharge the troops now in the service of the United States, except twenty-five privates to guard the stores at Fort Pitt and fifty-five to guard the stores at West Point and other magazines, with a proportionable number of officers, no officers to remain in service above the grade of captain.[9]

### The Army's Senior Officer a Captain

The guard detail at Fort Pitt was commanded by a genial lieutenant whose men proceeded to relieve the monotony of military service by getting themselves loaded during the Christmas holidays. Apparently deciding that the faithful old guns of the Revolution shouldn't be left out of the sport, they got a few artillery pieces loaded also. They wheeled out the guns and started blazing away into the night. Order was restored only after some brisk skirmishing in the streets. The surgeon dressed a few superficial wounds; the

---

[9] Although this declaration has been widely quoted by authorities, including Ganoe, I am told by Major A. P. Wade of the military history department at West Point that it is not quite correct. Elbridge Gerry of Massachusetts used this language in a speech before Congress, but the actual resolution did not contain his words in the form quoted above. Why did Congress disband 700 men and then raise 700 the next day? Major Wade explains that "the troops now in the service of the United States" were Henry Jackson's Regiment of Foot and two companies of the Corps of Artillery under Major Sebastian Bauman. Most of them were from Massachusetts and New Hampshire and were entitled to double pay. New York objected to the Massachusetts troops because of boundary jealousies. Congress wanted to do away with the double-pay status. The gimmick of disbanding one day and "rebanding" the next day was an easy solution to both problems.

principal tactical commanders were locked up; and two officers were temporarily relieved of command.

The rest of the Army behaved itself better at West Point. Perhaps it was due to the presence there of the senior American Army officer remaining in service: Captain (if you please) John Doughty.[10]

### The Eight Oldest U. S. Infantry Regiments

Although many American militia regiments date from the Revolution and some from colonial times, the oldest existing Regular Army regiment can trace its lineage only as far back as 1784.

A unit's "official lineage" is established by a rather intricate process. At the risk of oversimplification, here is a brief explanation of how our eight oldest regiments trace their military pedigrees.

Congress had no sooner abolished the Army as a menace to the "liberties of free people" when it realized that it would be convenient to have a few soldiers around to take care of foreign enemies. The British had refused to give up some of their western posts. Migration into the Ohio Valley was being challenged by the Indians—who were getting British help.

So in August of 1784 the "First American Regiment" was organized as "militia in the service of the U.S." It was commanded by Josiah Harmar whose grade at that time was "Lieutenant Colonel Commandant." Strung out along the Ohio River, it had the mission of guarding the frontier.

In October, 1790, the Indians had become so troublesome that Harmar's outfit was ordered out on a punitive expedition. The villages of the Miami Indians were destroyed. However, when the enraged Indians attacked the First American Regiment, the militia bugged out and left the few regulars in the outfit to their fate. The American "Army" had suffered its first defeat.

Congress did not see that the real lesson was the unreliability of militia—a song General Washington had sung throughout the Revolution. A second regiment was raised for a second "punitive expedition," but, due to a lack of enlistments, it too was composed for the most part of militia. Under command of General Arthur St.

[10] From *The Beginning of the U. S. Army,* by J. R. Jacobs (Princeton: Princeton University Press, 1947).

Clair, this force sallied forth into the wilderness and suffered the worst defeat ever sustained by U. S. troops: out of 1,400 effectives, 632 were killed and 264 wounded.[11] This, incidentally, led to the first "Congressional investigation." Congress finally realized that it needed a few "real" soldiers. General "Mad Anthony" Wayne, a distinguished Revolutionary War veteran, was brought back to command a new combined force of infantry, artillery and cavalry. The Legion of the United States, as it was called, was to consist of 5,120 men divided into four sublegions. Each sublegion was composed of eight infantry companies, four companies of riflemen, one company of artillery and one troop of dragoons. This organization of "combined arms" was the forerunner of our World War II Regimental Combat Teams (a concept "invented" almost four centuries earlier by Jan Zizka).

With Washington's backing, General Wayne did not immediately herd his new outfit into the woods to meet the punishment of the two earlier expeditions. For two years he trained his recruits. Then he moved a disciplined outfit against the Indians and destroyed them August 20, 1794, at the Battle of Fallen Timbers.[12]

The Legion of the United States had opened the way for westward expansion. As soon as Britain saw that the new nation had got around to raising a respectable military force, she honored her treaty obligations to abandon the northwestern posts forthwith. Communications in those days, however, were slow; it was not until 1796 that the Legion raised the American flag over the former British posts at Fort Miamis (Maumee, Ohio) and Detroit.

Congress then abolished the Legion. The four sublegions became the First, Second, Third and Fourth Infantry Regiments. Other regiments were authorized, partially raised and abolished during the next few years in the struggle of Congress between foreign threats and (what Jacobs [13] so aptly calls) its own "pathological fear of standing armies."

[11] Randolph G. Adams, *Lexington to Fallen Timbers,* University of Michigan Press, 1942.

[12] So called because it took place at a spot where a cyclone had left a wide swath of fallen trees. The Indians, who liked the area because of the cover it afforded them for their sniping tactics, were routed when "Mad Anthony" ordered his men to go after them with fixed bayonets!

[13] *Op. cit.*

By 1814 the infantry branch of the Army consisted of forty-eight infantry regiments numbered from the First through the Forty-eighth, and four rifle regiments numbered First through Fourth.[14] But in 1815 the Congressional meat cleaver came out again and started hacking up the Army. It is from the Congressional mayhem of 1815 that we get the peculiar lineage system that has been officially adopted.

Here is what happened. Congress ordered eight new regiments formed from the ruins of the fifty in existence. With no respect for tradition, the old regiments that happened to be closest together were pooled, reorganized into eight new regiments and given numbers in accordance with the seniority of the colonel who happened to command them at that time!

As a result:

1st Infantry was consolidated from the former 2d, 3d, 7th and 44th.
2d Infantry—from the 6th, 16th, 22d, 23d and 32d.
3d Infantry—from the 1st, 5th, 17th, 19th and 28th.
4th Infantry—from the 14th, 18th, 20th, 36th and 38th.
5th Infantry—from the 4th, 9th, 13th, 21st, 40th and 46th.
6th Infantry—from the 11th, 25th, 27th, 29th and 37th.
7th Infantry—from the 8th, 24th and 39th.
8th Infantry—from the 10th and 12th.[15]

The present Third Infantry (The Old Guard) is, therefore, the Army's oldest regiment by the accident of having absorbed the old First Infantry which, in turn, traces its lineage back to the "First American Regiment" of 1784.

No Regular Army *regiment* can trace its lineage beyond 1784, as we have already pointed out. The reason is simply that Congress, in abolishing the Continental Army that year, broke the direct lines of descent from Revolutionary War regiments to present-day regiments. Despite this fact, some unit historians make the false as-

---

[14] John K. Mahon, "History of the Organization of the United States Infantry," in *The Army Lineage Book;* vol. II (Infantry, Washington, 1953).

[15] Army style prescribes Arabic numerals for numbering regiments; Roman numerals for corps; and figures spelled out for armies and army groups. Except in the above regimental designations, a style more familiar to the civilian reader has been used.

sumption that their outfits can claim descent from any Revolutionary War unit having the same number.

## Oldest Regular Army *Units*

Only one unit was left in existence when Congress reduced the Army to eighty men in 1784. It is due to this accident that Battery D, Fifth Field Artillery Battalion, can trace its lineage to the Revolution and claim the distinction of being the oldest unit of the Regular Army.

"Alexander Hamilton's Provincial Company of Artillery of the Colony of New York" was organized in 1776. Survivors of this unit were included in Captain Doughty's 55-man guard detachment at West Point in 1784 (see above). In 1821 this unit was designated Battery F, Fourth Regiment of Artillery. In subsequent Army reorganizations its name was changed to the one it now bears: Battery D, Fifth Field Artillery Battalion.

It is interesting to note that this is one of only two D Batteries left in the Field Artillery today—since other Field Artillery battalions now have only three "lettered companies," "D" is not used. (Antiaircraft battalions, however, have four gun batteries.)

The unit in which former President Harry S. Truman served during World War I is the second exception. Known as "Truman's Battery," it has received special authority to retain its old designation of Battery D, 129th F. A. Battalion.

## The "Old Guard"

The Third Infantry, which traces its lineage through the Legion of the United States to the First American Regiment of 1784, is the oldest *regiment* of the Regular Army still in existence. Since 1948 it has been on duty at the nation's capital where (among other missions) it guards the Tomb of the Unknown Soldier, provides special security missions for the President, and furnishes honor guards for important American and foreign dignitaries.

The "Old Guard" has several interesting distinctions.

First, it is one of only two U. S. regiments that do not wear the usual type of unit distinctive insignia. The Third wears the unique "knapsack strap." This is officially described as "a black leather strap one-half inch wide with bull leather strap one-fourth inch wide woven in the middle—a simulation of the old buff and black knapsack strap. (To be worn on the left shoulder of the . . . coat and overcoat at the junction of the sleeve and shoulder. . . .)" [16]

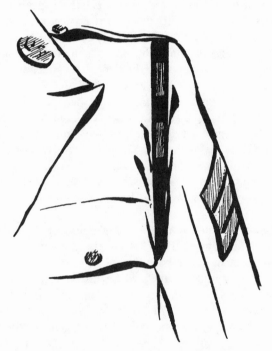

Regimental insignia of the Third Infantry.

I had just left the command of Company E, Third Infantry, to attend a service school when my "knapsack strap" got me into an amusing exchange of words with a brother officer who was among the uninitiated in Army tradition. He had never seen the strap before, and it obviously annoyed him. Finally, he asked what it was. "That's the regimental insignia of the Third Infantry," I said,

[16] The Fourth Infantry is the other regiment that does not wear the usual metal regimental insignia. Instead, it wears "a strip of scarlet cloth or ribbon one and one-half inches in width with a green stripe one-half inch in width in the center thereof; to be made into a band to fit the shoulder loop of the coat." As indicated by the colors, it dates from the Mexican War.

leading him on. "Oh? Something you boys thought up yourselves?" "As a matter of fact, yes," I answered, ". . . about a hundred and fifty years ago."

The origin of the strap, although not known, probably does go back a century and a half. One story is that prior to an early battle (possibly Lundy's Lane, 1814), members of the regiment wove strips of rawhide into the black leather shoulder straps of their knapsacks as a means of battlefield identification. After the battle a British prisoner of war commented that the Americans would not have won the day if it hadn't been for the devils with the distinctive knapsack straps. This is the stuff of which tradition is made. The regiment requested and was granted official permission to retain its distinctive marking—now conventionalized to its present form. Since regulations prescribe only one distinctive marking for a regiment, the "knapsack strap" then took the place of the metal insignia later adopted by all other regiments except the Fourth.

The Third Infantry is the only regiment permitted to use the "bordure of the United States" (the U. S. shield) in its coat of arms. This is in further recognition of its seniority.

Marching in parades with fixed bayonets is another distinctive privilege of the Third Infantry. This commemorates its attack on Telegraph Hill in the Battle of Cerro Gordo, 1847 (Mexican War).

The "Chapultepec Baton," which the regiment still possesses, was presented in 1848. Made from the original flagstaff of the Grand Plaza in Mexico City in 1847, it commemorates the regiment's decisive part in capturing the city. It has been told that a member of the regimental band participated in the assault on the critical fortress of Chapultepec with no weapon but his drum major's baton. The baton figures as one of the "supports" in the regiment's coat of arms.

Its nickname "The Old Guard" goes back to the Mexican War. When the Third Infantry approached the reviewing stand during the victory parade in Mexico City, General Winfield Scott took off his hat and said to his staff, "Gentlemen, remove your hats for the Old Guard of the Army."

The history of the Third Infantry Regiment is also a striking illustration of the American disregard for military tradition. Up until this century, the Third had one of the most outstanding battle records in our Army. Battle streamers on the regimental colors read like an outline of American military history—up until World War I. The regiment participated in every major engagement of the Mexican War and the Civil War. After Bull Run, General McDowell credited it with saving the Union "by its gallant conduct, unflinching steadiness and perfect order in covering the flight of the panic-stricken army."

Yet the Third Infantry was not permitted to fight in World War I, World War II or Korea! In 1946 this famous regiment was *deactivated,* along with units formed temporarily for World War II. It was a year and a half before this crime was discovered and partially atoned for. In April, 1948, in a ceremony at the United States Capitol Plaza in Washington, the "Old Guard" was resurrected.

## WEST POINT—1802

George Washington, although not a professional soldier himself, was outspoken about the unreliability of militia troops and amateur officers. Just two days before his death he wrote to Alexander Hamilton that the establishment of a military academy in America "upon a respectable and extensive basis, has ever been considered by me as an object of primary importance to this country; and while I was in the Chair of Government, I omitted no opportunity of recommending it, in my public speeches and other ways, to the attention of the Legislature."

On July 4, 1802, the United States Military Academy opened at West Point with ten cadets present.

As surprising as it may seem, the USMA is one of the world's oldest military schools. France's famous cavalry school, Saumur, dates back to the eighteenth century; but Saint Cyr was not founded until 1808.[17] France's École Polytechnique was established only eight years before West Point. England's Royal Military Academy

---

[17] Madame de Maintenon, mistress and second wife of Louis XIV, started a school at Saint Cyr in 1684 for the daughters of impoverished noblemen. She is buried in the chapel there. The military school at Saint Cyr, established by Napoleon, was destroyed in World War II and now is temporarily located in Brittany.

at Woolwich was founded in 1741; the Royal Military College at Sandhurst was established the same year as West Point.

For many years West Point was the only engineering school in America. Until after the Civil War, it was the graduates of West Point who led explorations of the West, surveyed routes for roads and railroads, built bridges, tunnels, ports and directed most of the civil engineering work in the country. The United States Corps of Engineers, into which West Point's top graduates traditionally go, is still charged with much of the country's civil engineering works.

In the Mexican War, Washington's foresight in pressing for the establishment of an American military academy paid off dramatically. In the words of General Winfield Scott:

> I give it as my fixed opinion, that but for our graduated cadets, the war between the United States and Mexico might, and probably would, have lasted some four or five years, with, in its first half, more defeats than victories falling to our share; whereas, in less than two campaigns we conquered a great country and a peace, without the loss of a single battle or skirmish.

In the Union Army, West Pointers started in subordinate capacities but rose rapidly as the ineptitude of politically appointed generals was revealed in combat. By 1865 all general officers of the Federal line were graduates. In every major engagement of the Civil War, West Pointers commanded the forces on at least one side, and usually on both sides.

In World War I, all army commanders of the American Expeditionary Force and all but four of the thirty-eight corps and division commanders were West Pointers.

In World War II, although West Pointers constituted less than two per cent of all officers in the Army, eighty-three per cent of the four-star generals, sixty-five per cent of the three-star generals and fifty-five per cent of the two-star generals were graduates.

Not many people realize how few officers West Point has produced. In slightly over a century and a half of operation, only about 20,000 men have worn the West Point class ring. It is interesting to note that almost half of that number—8,000—saw active service in World War II. This is because the early West Point classes were extremely small. Approximately 600 officers a year are now graduated.[18]

## The West Point Class Ring

Class rings, now worn by graduates of most schools, are almost certainly a West Point innovation.

The USMA Class of 1835 was the first to wear West Point "class rings." They were massive gold things which bore a drum and cannon on one side and a shot and sword on the other. The stone was amethyst, in the form of a shield, and engraved with the class seal. There was no class ring the next year (so far as is known). But each class from 1837 until the present has had a ring.

Before 1869, every member of the class designed his own ring. Starting in 1869, each class has appointed a Ring Committee to select a uniform design. Until 1917 the rings were made by hand. After that date the West Point classes were so increased in size that the rings were made from dies.

Contrary to common belief, all rings of a given graduating class do not have the same stone—each cadet selects his own setting. All rings since World War I are of the same general design—of massive gold, with "West Point" and the year of graduation circling the stone, the Academy shield on one side and the individual class shield on the other. Each class, however, makes individual arrangements with a jeweler for its rings.

It is traditional for class rings to be distributed to the senior ("First") class before graduation. Cadets wear their rings on the third finger of the left hand with the class shield toward the heart until graduation. After graduation the ring is reversed so that the Academy shield is toward the heart.

## Ex-Cadet Edgar Allan Poe

One of the most distinguished nongraduates of West Point is Edgar Allan Poe.

However, it was not indifference to military life or inaptitude that led to Poe's dismissal in 1831 after approximately seven

[18] Annapolis is considerably larger with an enrollment of about 3,600 as compared with approximately 2,500 at West Point.

months' service as a cadet. Actually, Poe appeared to have been very much a "soldier at heart" even after his dismissal.

Before entering the University of Virginia, Edgar Allan Poe had belonged to the cadet corps in Richmond. He enlisted in the Army after graduating from the University and did so well that he was promoted to regimental sergeant major within a few months.

His stepfather, Mr. Allan, got him an appointment to West Point and bought his discharge from the Army so that he might enter. He was doing all right as a cadet, but got into a controversy with his stepfather about money. Apparently with a resolve to rid himself of financial dependence on Mr. Allan, Poe decided to leave West Point and support himself by writing poetry.

His method of terminating connections with West Point was simply to refuse to attend formations. It worked, and he was duly thrown out.

The story is that when the uniform for parade was announced as "white belts and gloves, under arms," the poetic Poe showed up stark naked except for white belts, gloves and his rifle. This tale would appear to be made from the whole cloth.

No hard feelings were harbored on either side. Quite the contrary. Colonel Sylvanus Thayer, the "Father of the Military Academy," and then Superintendent, authorized the cadets to subscribe seventy-five cents each from their meager Cadet Store accounts for the publication of a collection of Poe's poems in 1831. The volume, known as "the West Point edition" bears the following inscription: "To the U. S. Corps of Cadets this volume is respectfully dedicated." It includes the first publication of *To Helen, Israfel* and *Lenore.*

The library at West Point has remembered ex-Cadet Edgar Allan Poe with a memorial door which includes the following from Sir Francis Bacon:

> "There is no exquisite beauty without
> "Some strangeness in the proportion."

### James McNeill Whistler—ex-1855

"If silicon were a gas I would be a major general now," Whistler used to say in his later years. He was "found deficient" in chemistry.

There is an anecdote about Whistler's cadet service which is so good it has to be told—even if it probably isn't true. The drawing instruction was naturally a snap for Cadet Whistler. The assignment one day was to copy a picture of a stone bridge. Whistler finished way ahead of his classmates and, to while away the rest of the allotted time, sketched in a couple of small boys fishing from the rail of the bridge. The instructor, making his rounds, spotted the doodling and ordered the boys removed from the bridge. The next time he came around the two boys had been neatly erased from the bridge and were fishing from the bank. This time the instructions were explicit: "Mr. Whistler! I want those two boys removed entirely."

On his next tour the instructor found two little tombstones at the spot where the boys had been sitting.

In the West Point library is a series of Whistler's sketches showing a cadet on guard duty. The guard is first shown as the epitome of military alertness; in the final sketch he is asleep under a tree. Before he tangled with silicon, Whistler also drew the lithographed covers for several pieces of West Point music.

### Regimental Coats of Arms and Insignia

Back in the twelfth century, knights began to paint their shields with bold, brightly colored devices. This permitted them to be identified not only in battle but, more especially, in tournaments. "Heralds" were originally a species of sports announcer whose function it was to sound off the name and "record" of each contestant as he entered the lists. There being no printed programs in those days, it was a case of "ye can't tell ye contestants without a herald."

Of course the heralds became experts at identifying coats of arms. As the latter got more complicated, the need arose for some central authority to regulate their design and use. The heralds were naturally selected. They started drawing up rules and their art became known as "heraldry."

All U. S. Army regiments and separate battalions are authorized a coat of arms and a distinctive insignia. The coat of arms is embroidered on the color or standard; the insignia is worn on the shoulder strap of the uniform.[19]

In most cases, a unit's insignia is almost identical with its official coat of arms. Most insignia omit the crest of the coat of arms and add the motto.

Coats of arms for American units were not commonly in existence until after World War I. There is now a Heraldic Branch, Office of the Quartermaster General, which assists units in matters of heraldry and which gives official approval to designs.

Ancient rules of heraldry are still followed. After a little study, you can figure out the highlights of a regiment's history from its coat of arms. Indian wars, for example, are indicated by arrows tied in a rattlesnake skin (the Indian symbol for war). A bolo indicates service in the Philippines; a fleur-de-lis, service in France; a "white cross pattée," badge of the Army of the Potomac's V Corps, indicates Civil War service with that unit; a dragon indicates China service; an acorn, badge of the First Division of XIV Corps in the Civil War, symbolizes former membership in that unit. These are merely random illustrations from among many examples.

A common error is to say "crest" when you mean "coat of arms." The "crest" is the portion of the coat of arms above the shield. It so happens that some regiments use their crests as their "distinctive insignia" which is worn on the shoulder strap (e.g., Seventh and Thirty-first Infantries). In most instances, however, the "distinctive insignia" consists of the "shield" with the motto added. It is not correct to call this a "regimental crest," however much handier that tag is than "regimental distinctive insignia."

While we are on the subject, the next time you hear somebody use the expression "bar sinister" (signifying illegitimacy) you can make yourself thoroughly objectionable by pointing out that he means *"bend* sinister." As pointed out on page 27, in the discussion of chevrons, a "bar" is a *horizontal* line, so it can be neither "sinister" nor "dexter."

---

[19] Strictly speaking, the word is "insigne" in the singular and "insignia" in the plural. By common misusage, however, "insignia" has come to serve for both singular and plural.

## THE ARMS AND SERVICES

### Birth Dates, Colors and Insignia

Color has long been used in armies for identification as well as decoration. Colored flags to distinguish military units were used as far back as the seventeenth century by Chinese armies as well as by the English. Yet the idea can be traced back to the days when Roman charioteers indicated their factions by wearing colored sashes; rivalry became so keen that fights between "Greens" and "Blues" carried beyond the arena. During the Middle Ages, colors became identified with certain virtues; bishops prescribed rules that gold represented honor, white indicated purity, blue meant truth, red stood for strength, etc.

Military leaders soon discovered that identifying certain types of troops with colors was a great aid to creating *esprit de corps*. Colors had to be assigned arbitrarily to many of the older arms and services. But some, such as the green of the Light Infantry, sprang up naturally: green had long been the color of the woodsman's clothing (for camouflage) and Light Infantry was organized originally from woodsmen and hunters. Although the Light Infantry mission has long since disappeared, green is still the color of British outfits that trace their lineage to these units.

In America, as far back as the Revolution, infantry units wore white metal buttons and insignia; artillery wore gold-colored ornaments. (We were slow in developing true cavalry, so they were not always present in our early armies.) About 1850, colors were prescribed for all American arms and services.

The information given below is for the Army's twelve "basic branches." These are listed in order of their official seniority, as determined by the Office, Chief of Military History. Since there is so much confusion over the terms "branch," "service," "arm," "component," "technical and administrative service," an attempt to explain this rather complicated matter is presented in Appendix C.

INFANTRY   Established June 14, 1775. Light blue.

The crossed-rifle insignia was adopted in 1875. Until 1924 there was an attempt made to keep the insignia up to date by changing rifle models. Present design features the original U. S. Army musket.

ADJUTANT GENERAL'S CORPS   Established June 16, 1775. Dark blue and scarlet.

Insignia design authorized in 1872.

CORPS OF ENGINEERS   Established June 16, 1775. Scarlet and white.

The castle insignia was adopted in 1840. The office of Chief of Engineers was established June 16, 1776. A Corps of Engineers existed from March 11, 1779, until 1783. On May 9, 1794, a "Corps of Artillerists and Engineers" was established; it was abolished March 16, 1802, when the present Corps of Engineers was organized.

FINANCE CORPS   Established June 16, 1775. Silver-gray and golden yellow.

The present insignia, a diamond, was originally used by the Pay Corps. It disappeared during the years 1912 (approximately) to 1920. The diamond has been used since 1920, when the Pay Corps was combined with the Quartermaster Corps.

QUARTERMASTER CORPS   Established June 16, 1775. Buff.

The crossed saber and key on a wheel, surmounted by an eagle, was adopted in 1896.

ARTILLERY   Established July 21, 1775. Scarlet.

Crossed-cannon insignia was first authorized in 1836. After 1901 the Coast Artillery used an insignia consisting of the crossed cannon with a red enamel oval bearing a projectile pointing upward; this was superimposed in the center. Between 1901 and 1907 the Field Artillery insignia included a wheel on an oval in the center of the crossed cannon. For many years there were three distinct types of artillery: Field, Coast and Antiaircraft. After World War II they were consolidated into one branch with the same crossed cannon insignia and the same color (scarlet).

ARMOR   Cavalry was established December 12, 1776. Yellow.

Crossed sabers were adopted in 1851 and worn until 1950. After World War II the Cavalry was abolished (1950) and it was officially decreed that "The Armor shall be the continuation of the Cavalry." The crossed sabers were modified by superimposing an

M-26 tank. The Armored Force had formerly used green and yellow as its colors; its insignia had been prescribed in 1942 as an M-VIII tank.

ORDNANCE CORPS  Established May 14, 1812. Crimson and yellow.

Adopted in 1832, from a model long used in foreign armies, this "flaming bomb" is the oldest U. S. military service insignia.

SIGNAL CORPS  Established June 21, 1860. Orange and white.

Ours was the first army in history to have a "signal corps." Crossed signal flags were first worn as insignia by enlisted men on the sleeve. In 1884 the torch was added.

CHEMICAL CORPS  Established June 28, 1918. Cobalt blue and golden yellow.

The "benzene ring" on crossed retorts was adopted in World War I.

MILITARY POLICE CORPS  Established September 26, 1941. Yellow and green.

The MP insignia is crossed pistols of the "Harpers Ferry" model.

TRANSPORTATION CORPS  Established July 31, 1942. Brick red and golden yellow.

The insignia was created in 1942 by the addition of a shield and ship's wheel to the insignia of the World War I Transportation Corps. (The Transportation Division, QMGO, was established July 18, 1898.)

### OTHER DISTINCTIVE COLORS

| | |
|---|---|
| General Staff Corps | Gold and black |
| Inactive Reserve | Brown and white |
| Military Intelligence Reserve | Golden yellow and purple |
| National Guard Bureau | Dark blue |
| Specialists' Reserve | Brown and golden yellow |
| U. S. Military Academy Professors | Scarlet and silver-gray |
| Warrant Officers | Brown |
| Cap "piping" (cord-edge braid) | |
| General officers | Gold |
| All other commissioned officers | Gold and black |
| Warrant officers | Black and silver |

## Segregated and Other Special Outfits

Most units in our early wars were made up of men and officers from the same state. The earliest units composed of men more directly linked to the Federal government than to any particular state were two regiments of United States Sharpshooters (First and Second), organized in 1861. Their most distinguishing feature was that their officers were appointed by the Federal government.

A total of 138 regiments of colored infantry were organized during the course of the Civil War. With the exception of two Massachusetts regiments, all Negro regiments were finally mustered directly into Federal service and organized and officered under the authority of the United States. These troops first bore the exotic name of "Corps d'Afrique." By the spring of 1864 they were known as United States Colored Troops.

The four regiments of the Indian Home Guards (designated the First through the Fourth) were also organized during the Civil War and handled in the same manner as the colored regiments.

Another interesting Civil War Federal volunteer outfit was the Invalid Corps. Established in 1863 and classed as infantry, it was composed of men who had become physically unfit for combat. Those who could handle a weapon and make light marches were put in the First Battalion and used as nurses and cooks around hospitals. Many able-bodied men were freed for combat by the use of the twenty-four regiments and 188 separate companies of invalids who did duty. (This Invalid Corps bears a strong similarity to the German World War II "Organization Todt," composed of "invalids" who did construction work and other logistical tasks in accordance with their physical capabilities.) Since the initials of the Invalid Corps coincided unfortunately with the "Inspected-Condemned" stamped on worn-out government equipment, the name was changed to Veteran Reserve Corps.

In 1864, Confederate prisoners of war were organized into six infantry regiments of United States Volunteers (First through Sixth) for frontier service. They were given missions that did not involve fighting against the Confederacy.

During the war with Spain, units were made up of men from another special group—the "immunes." Five regiments of whites and five of Negroes (each consisting of just under 1,000 enlisted men) were composed of men "immune" to tropical diseases (i.e., Southerners).[20]

In 1899, Filipino companies were organized and paid as civilian employees of the Quartermaster. In 1901 they were officially organized into fifty companies, officered from the Regular Army except for the lieutenants, who could be natives. These companies were organized into thirteen battalions between 1904 and 1917. During World War I these became parts of five regiments, the Forty-third, Forty-fourth, Forty-fifth, Fifty-seventh and Sixty-second.

A Puerto Rican battalion, formed in 1899, was combined with a battalion of mounted infantry in 1901 to form a regiment. It later (1920) became the Sixty-fifth Infantry, which was part of the Third Division in Korea.

The Twenty-fourth and Twenty-fifth Infantry Regiments were constituted in Louisiana in 1866 and composed of Negro personnel from that date until after World War II when they were both inactivated. (The Twenty-fourth was inactivated in 1951 in Pusan, Korea; the Twenty-fifth was broken up in 1950 and redesignated Twenty-fifth Armored Infantry Battalion in 1951.) The two Negro divisions, the Ninety-second and Ninety-third, have also been inactivated as have the two cavalry regiments, the Ninth and Tenth.

A special separate battalion was made up of Norwegian-Americans during World War II and marked for service in Scandinavia. Although this special mission was never performed, the Ninety-ninth distinguished itself in the fighting in Europe. In 1945 it was assigned to the hybrid 473d Infantry. The latter also included many men from the inactivated First Special Service Force, some from the First, Third and Fourth Ranger Battalions.

### "Go for Broke"

Units composed of Japanese-Americans in World War II probably brought more honor to American arms than any other United

---

. [20] My Louisiana grandfather, who served as a major in the Fourth U. S. Volunteers, "Hood's Immunes," was "immune" just long enough to reach Cuba and catch yellow fever. He recovered to command a battalion, the sergeant major of which was Walter Kreuger.

States unit in our entire military history. These "soldiers of an enemy race" were formed first into the 100th Infantry Battalion (June, 1942) composed of Hawaiian Nisei. After the 100th Battalion went to Italy, the 442d Infantry Regiment was organized at Camp Shelby, Mississippi, with "American citizens of Japanese ancestry having resided in the United States since birth." The 442d furnished replacements to the 100th Battalion until the 442d arrived in Italy and completed the team. The "Go for Broke" [21] regiment so distinguished itself in Italy and France that it has been allowed to retain its designation. It is now allotted to the Army Reserve and located in Hawaii (Oahu, T. H.)

### Why No J Company?

There is a considerable amount of unfounded folklore as to why our Army has no J companies. The most romantic story is that J companies did once exist but one of them so thoroughly disgraced itself that the designation was abolished. This is sheer fabrication. Another hot-stove hypothesis is that we have no J companies because the Roman Army had none. The only thing wrong with this theory is that the Romans didn't have any A, B, C, D or any other lettered companies either. Roman companies (which they called centuries) were numbered.

The American Army started lettering its companies in 1816. Since the script "J" looked so much like "I" the letter J was not used. (J is the most recent addition to our alphabet and when first adopted was used interchangeably with I. Remember also that the Army of that day relied entirely on handwritten orders and correspondence which made the likelihood even greater that the I's and J's would be confused.)

Up until 1816 the standard regiment consisted of ten companies.[22] In the early days the regiment and battalion were identical.

[21] Island slang for "Give it your all."

[22] This statement is somewhat oversimplified. Harmar's Regiment in 1784 (see above) had ten companies, but two of them were artillery. In 1787 the infantry regiment consisted of eight companies and the artillery was organized—on paper, at least—as a battalion. Between 1791 and 1796 the regiment was supposed to consist of twelve companies (organized into three battalions). From 1799 until 1816 the standard regiment (battalion) had ten companies.

Eight of the ten companies were known as "battalion companies." Following the British pattern, the other two were elite or "flank companies." (One of these the British called the "Grenadier Company" and filled it with men picked for their strength and courage. Sometimes the grenadier companies were detached from their regiments and used together in provisional grenadier battalions [e.g., at Bunker Hill]. The other flank company was called the "Light Company." They were used as skirmishers ahead of the main line. They too were often detached and used in provisional battalions. The Americans did not organize any "grenadier" companies; both "flank companies" were light infantry. Lafayette commanded the Corps of Light Infantry in 1780 and under him it made the chief assaults on Yorktown the next year.)

The eight "battalion companies" up until 1816 did not have permanent number designations. "For training and for battle purposes, the eight battalion companies were placed in line by a complex arrangement according to the seniority of their captains, which seems to have had its origin in the protocol of medieval armies. It had no functional basis, since once lined up, the companies were renumbered from right to left." [23]

Under the new 1816 system, the two flank companies got the letters A and B, and the others C through K. Mahon confirms the theory that "There was no J Company because J was too easily confused with I in writing." [24]

## EVOLUTION OF RANK INSIGNIA

Several stories have been fabricated to explain the origin and the reason for adopting our present system of insignia to denote the rank of officers in the American Army. One peculiarity of our system is that silver takes precedence over gold in insignia. (We shall see the reason in a moment.) The other is that our insignia differ markedly from those in foreign armies. Up until the time of our Revolutionary War, officers did not wear insignia of rank in

[23] John K. Mahon, "History of the Organization of United States Infantry," in *The Army Lineage Book,* vol. II (Infantry, Washington, 1953).

[24] "J" Company did exist in at least one administrative regiment (Military Government) during World War II.

the sense we know them now. Officers were distinguished by different types of uniform or by special markings on their uniforms.

In the early stages of the American Revolution it became apparent that some means of identifying officers in our Army was necessary. As an expedient, field officers were ordered to wear red cockades on their hats, captains wore yellow or buff and lieutenants were provided with cockades of green.

In 1780, Washington recommended that major generals wear epaulettes with two stars on each shoulder; brigadier generals would also wear two epaulettes with one star on each; field grade officers would wear a plain gold epaulette on each shoulder; captains, one epaulette on the right shoulder and subalterns would wear one on the left.[25] Sergeants would wear a worsted shoulder knot on each shoulder and corporals would wear one on the right. This system was put into effect in 1782.

When the rank of lieutenant general was created, three stars were prescribed. An interesting sidelight here is the fact that Washington was technically not a "full general"—it was not until the Civil War that this grade appeared (Grant, Sherman and Sheridan).

When the Army was reorganized in 1821, the chevron was adopted as a means of denoting rank for company grade officers as well as noncommissioned officers. Captains wore one chevron above the elbow: lieutenants one below. A few years later this was abolished (1832) and the spread eagle was adopted as the insignia for full colonels.

At this time it became the practice for all officers to wear epaulettes. Infantry officers wore silver ones and all others wore gold. So that insignia of rank would be clearly visible on these epaulettes, they were of opposite colors—an infantry colonel wore a gold eagle on his silver epaulette, and other colonels wore silver eagles on gold.

A few years later (1836) the shoulder strap replaced the epaulette on field uniforms. It had a border of silver or gold depending on the color of the epaulette it replaced; the interior was the same color as the uniform facings. The leaf and the bars appeared at this

[25] The last idea must have come from the British who tried the same thing about this time and soon abandoned it. (James Laver, *British Military Uniforms* [London: Penguin Books, 1948.])

time as insignia of rank but the colors were not fixed—officers wore gold insignia on silver-bordered shoulder straps and vice versa.

Starting in 1851 all epaulettes and shoulder strap borders were gold; rank insignia for all arms became the same color. On the epaulettes all insignia were silver. Majors and second lieutenants, however, wore no rank insignia—they were distinguished only by the type of fringe on their epaulettes. Rank insignia on shoulder straps were silver for all officers down to and including lieutenant colonels; captains and first lieutenants wore gold insignia.

### Why Silver "Ranks" Gold

When epaulettes were abolished from the uniforms of regimental officers in 1872 and replaced with shoulder knots which had no fringes, it became necessary to devise some insignia for the major to distinguish him from the second lieutenant. So the gold leaf was adopted to denote majors. This is why the lieutenant colonel has a silver insignia and the major wears gold. At the same time that this change was taking place, the color of the bars of junior officers on shoulder straps was changed to silver. The second lieutenant wore no insignia and was distinguished only by the shoulder strap or knot.

The need for insignia to denote the rank of second lieutenant first became apparent when the Army adopted khaki uniforms in the Spanish-American War and officers and men alike wore plain shoulder straps. But it was not until 1917 that the Army decided to adopt a new insignia for him. The plan which would call for the least possible change was to follow the color precedent established in devising the major's insignia and adopt the gold bars.

Full generals are permitted to choose their own insignia of rank. General Pershing, the first full general since the Civil War, chose four stars and his precedent was followed by the other two full generals of that war—Peyton March and Tasker Bliss. The five-star rank was created in World War II.

### ORIGIN OF AMERICAN MILITARY DECORATIONS

Our country was very slow in establishing a system of military decorations. This may well have been deliberate. Foreign armies had decorations and we have always been reluctant to adopt anything "foreign" that might glamorize the soldier.

Washington had the military perspicacity to see the need for decorations and had the "Purple Heart" created in 1782. It was to be a decoration for "singularly meritorious action" and consisted of a small heart in purple cloth to be worn on the tunic over the left breast. Three of them were awarded in 1783, but the records show no others.

The soldier became popular again in 1847 when we were fighting in Mexico. At this time a thing known as a "Certificate of Merit" was created. It was simply a document—there was no medal or ribbon to go with it. Later Congress provided that holders of the certificate who were still in service should have extra pay of two dollars per month. This award, however, was a decisive step forward and indicated that public view toward the soldier was softening.

The next step in the evolution of American decorations was the "brevet" system of promotion. This was a means of honoring soldiers for gallantry by granting a "brevet rank" higher than his actual rank and giving him the insignia to go with it. However, this system fell victim to political abuses and by the time the Civil War started it had become meaningless.[26]

In December of 1861, Senator James W. Grimes of Iowa, as chairman of the Senate Naval Committee, introduced a bill that resulted in the establishment of a Medal of Honor for enlisted men of the Navy. This is the first decoration formally authorized by the American government to be worn as a badge of honor.

Action on an Army medal was started two months later when Senator Henry Wilson of Massachusetts introduced into the Senate a resolution providing for presentations of "medals of honor" to enlisted men of the Army and the Voluntary Forces who "shall most distinguish themselves by their gallantry in action and other soldier-like qualities." This became law July 12, 1862. It was amended March 3, 1863, to include officers and made retroactive

[26] This section is based on *Orders, Decorations and Insignia*, by Colonel (later Brigadier General) Robert E. Wyllie (New York: G. P. Putnam's Sons, 1921).

to the beginning of the Civil War. This legislation was the basis for the award until 1918, when it was completely revised.

The criteria for presenting the Medal of Honor were very much lower in our early wars than they are now. It was not until 1902 that steps were taken to establish lesser awards so that the Medal of Honor would be "protected" from presentation for any other than the most severe tests of heroism.

Army Medals of Honor presented in wars up to 1918 were as follows:

| | | |
|---|---|---:|
| 1861-1865 | (Civil War) | 1,200 |
| 1861-1898 | (Indian Campaigns) | 416 |
| 1898 | (War with Spain) | 30 |
| 1899-1913 | (Philippine Insurrection) | 70 |
| 1900 | (Boxer Rebellion) | 4 |
| 1911 | (Mexican Campaign) | 1 |

The Distinguished Service Cross (DSC) was established in 1918 for "extraordinary heroism in military operations against an armed enemy" under circumstances not deserving award of the Medal of Honor. Between World Wars I and II a "pyramid" of fifteen distinct awards for valor and merit was set up with the Medal of Honor at the top. Army Medals of Honor since 1911 have been awarded in the following numbers:

| | | |
|---|---|---:|
| 1918 | (World War I) | 95 |
| 1922-1935 | (Unknown soldiers, Lindbergh, Greeley) | 8 |
| 1942-1945 | (World War II) | 292 |
| 1950-1953 | (Korea) | 71 |
| | Total Medals of Honor | 2,187 |

Five men have won two Medals of Honor. In 1918 the regulations were changed to prevent any one person's getting it more than once.

Although awarded "In the name of Congress," this decoration is properly known as the "Medal of Honor," not the "Congressional Medal of Honor."

The initial Army order (from William Wilson & Son, Philadelphia) in 1862 was for 2,000 of the Medals of Honor. This is less than 200 medals short of the number issued through 1954.

As a leftover, probably, from the 1847 "Certificate of Merit," there is a regulation which entitles enlisted men still in military service who hold the Medal of Honor to an additional two dollars per month pay.

Former soldiers who have won the Medal of Honor are entitled to an annual pension of $120 on reaching the age of sixty-five. Holders of the nation's highest award are also allowed free military air transportation under certain conditions. There is no basis to the myth that enlisted Medal of Honor holders are entitled to a salute from officers. (See also page 151.)

The two dollars per month also goes to enlisted holders of the Distinguished Service Cross (DSC), Distinguished Service Medal (DSM), Distinguished Flying Cross (DFC) or Soldier's Medal. This privilege does not apply to the Silver Star, although the latter (authorized in 1932) is a higher award for valor than the DFC and SM, and ranks the same as the DFC for merit.

### Campaign Medals

Campaign medals and their ribbons were not authorized for United States Armed Forces until 1905.

The Army now has twenty-four service medals starting with the one for the Civil War (awarded retroactively) and extending through Korea. All of them are in the shape of a disk.

### First Medal of Honor Winners

The first man to perform a feat for which he was to be awarded the Medal of Honor was Colonel Bernard J. D. Irwin. Although he performed the feat in 1861, he was not decorated until 1894. (He died in Chicago in 1917.)

This is what he did. In what is now Arizona, an Apache band during a cattle raid kidnaped the son of one of the few frontier families. A rescue party from the Seventh Infantry was shot up and surrounded by the Indians. It managed to get a messenger back to Fort Breckenridge where Irwin was assistant surgeon. Knowing that several of the rescue party had been wounded, Irwin volunteered to lead a party of fourteen picked infantrymen to relieve the first group. Mounted on mules, the volunteers set off through a heavy snowstorm on February 13 and on the next night they drove off the Indians surrounding the would-be rescuers. After treating the wounded, Irwin found the Indian village and wiped it out.

The first Army Medals of Honor to be actually awarded were presented to six soldiers in a joint ceremony in 1863. They were the survivors of a twenty-two-man group of volunteers who had gone deep into enemy territory to cut the rail line that served as a vital Confederate supply link between Marietta, Georgia, and Chattanooga, Tennessee.

These men, disguised as civilians, left camp near Shelbyville, Tennessee, on the night of April 7, 1862, and drifted singly into Chattanooga. There they boarded the train for Marietta, spent the night of April 11, and on the next day bought tickets for a northbound train to the town of Big Shanty (now Kenesaw) eight miles north of Marietta.

Leader of this undertaking was a civilian secret agent named James J. Andrews, who had been planning it for months. Andrews had picked Big Shanty because of its isolation and lack of telegraphic connections with other stations on the line.

When the train stopped at Big Shanty the conductor shouted "twenty minutes for breakfast." Passengers and trainmen got off on the right-hand side of the train. Andrews and his raiders piled off the opposite side, climbed into the engine and took off. A few miles up the line they stopped, tore down telegraph wires and piled crossties on the track. Andrews gave his crew a final briefing and they continued the sabotaging journey. They had passed Calhoon with a clear track to Chattanooga when the Confederates took up the pursuit in another train.

As the other train gained on them, Andrews cut the end cars loose from his train one by one. This did not succeed as well as you might expect: the Confederate engineer would simply slow down, drive into the loose cars, and push them on ahead. Andrews finally had only one car left. He and his men broke this one open and dropped cross-ties out of the end onto the track. But this slowed down the pursuers only slightly. The saboteurs finally set fire to the last boxcar and let it loose as they crossed a long bridge at Oostenaula, leaving it burning in the middle of the bridge. The Confederate engineer was able to handle this also; slowing up, he eased into the burning car and rolled it on ahead until he could get rid of it in a siding.

After almost ninety miles of this melodramatic contest, the pirated locomotive ran out of fuel near Graysville. Andrews and his men took to the woods but all were rounded up within a few days. Andrews and seven of his men were tried and executed in Atlanta. The other fourteen stayed in prison until the following October when eight of them overwhelmed their guards and escaped. The remaining six were paroled almost a year after their exploit and became the first actually to receive the Medal of Honor. (The first of the six was Private Jacob Parrott.)

### The Irish and the Medal of Honor

Seventeen Murphys, ten Kellys and six Kelleys have won the nation's highest award for valor. The only name to rank the Murphys on the official list of Medal of Honor winners is "Smith" (with twenty-six names).

Four of the ten Kellys were named Thomas.

### The Last Battle with the Indians

At Wounded Knee Creek, South Dakota, in December, 1890, our Indian Wars came to an end.

This "battle," aside from its historical significance, is interesting as an example of what Indian fights were like.

The great Indian generals—Sitting Bull, Chief Joseph, Crazy Horse and Geronimo—had been defeated between 1877 and 1885. For a time it looked as if there would be no more trouble.

But in 1890 the Sioux tribes on their various reservations embarked on a semi-religious binge and their leaders started talking up the idea that an Indian Messiah was coming to lead them to final victory against the whites. Some 1,800 Sioux broke off the reservation and assembled in the Bad Lands where they whipped themselves up to a high pitch of fanaticism which involved vapor baths, fasting, "ghost dancing" and much oratory.

The government thought it a wise precaution to pick up Sitting Bull and take him into custody before the old chief could provide the leadership to turn this mob into a real military threat.

The lieutenant in charge of the command sent to arrest Sitting Bull was killed by the chief's followers the moment he announced his intentions. Two Indian police sergeants with the Federal forces immediately shot Sitting Bull. In the fracas that followed, many of the Indians escaped and made their way to Wounded Knee Creek where they joined forces with another Indian leader named Big Foot.

Colonel James W. Forsyth, leader of the expedition sent to capture them, surrounded the camp and asked for a parley. He hoped to disarm them peacefully. The Indians were sullen as they came out in their blankets for the powwow. When asked to turn over their weapons, they made a pretense of searching through their tepees but turned over only two rifles.

It was pretty obvious that a nasty incident was shaping up.

Forsyth ordered his men to search the tents and they produced fifty rifles. At this point one of the seated Indians pulled a hidden rifle from a blanket and fired. That did it.

For seven hours the fight raged through the Indian camp with no chance for orderly direction. It was every man for himself at first. Then the soldiers began to form into little units with their own leaders. A group of Indians found a ravine from which they poured fire on the troops. Second Lieutenant Hawthorne, commanding a platoon of the First Artillery, had two Hotchkiss howitzers which he moved forward on his own initiative—and at considerable personal risk—to bring devastating enfilade fire on the Indians in the ravine.

Infantry charged into the ravine and engaged the enemy in hand-to-hand combat. Hawthorne, though badly wounded, maintained command of his men and at the critical moment kept them from firing into the melee and hitting our own troops. (He and seventeen others won Medals of Honor in this action.) [27]

By 3 P.M. it was all over. The discipline and training of regular troops had enabled them to recover from their initial disorganization and carry the day against a crafty and courageous enemy.

Organized Indian resistance had finally been crushed.

[27] From *The Medal of Honor* (Washington, D. C.: Government Printing Office, 1948).

## Army Service Numbers

The use of "serial numbers" for enlisted men in the United States Army started in 1918. The system was prescribed later for officers. Serial Number 1 went to Arthur B. Cream, an old soldier in the Medical Department. The first serial number for officers was assigned to General John J. Pershing: "01."

Blocks of numbers have been allocated so that any particular number can belong to only one man. Although an individual's number can change (for example, an enlisted man will get a new number if he is commissioned), once a number is awarded it will never be assigned to another person. The term has recently been changed to "Army Service Number." General Douglas MacArthur's ASN is 057.

## Dog Tags

Although various types of identification tags were sold by commercial outfits during the Civil War, it was not until 1908 that the Army started issuing them. The first official "dog tags" were aluminum disks about the size of a half dollar. They were stamped with the name, rank and unit of the wearer.

After the adoption of serial numbers (1918), the tags included the number but omitted unit and rank.

The present tags are two by one and an eighth inches and made of a noncorrosive metal. They now include name, Army service number, record of tetanus immunization, blood type and religious preference.

Religious preference was formerly indicated only as C (Roman Catholic), J (Jewish), P (Protestant), X (for any other group that would not come under one of the previous headings) or Y (if the individual did not designate). A regulation of 1956 (AR 606-5) prescribes that in lieu of the "X" the tag will *specify* the religion. The "Y" is replaced by the statement "no preference."

Veterans of North Africa and Italy during World War II can tell you dog-tag stories about the British Gurkhas and the French "Goumiers." These fierce colonial troops, fabulous patrol experts, learned to feel for the shape of dog tags when they came on sleeping soldiers of whose identity they were not sure. Many a startled

American awoke with a knife at his throat and lay paralyzed with
terror while the Gurkha or Goumier felt for his dog tag to see
whether he would slit his throat for a German or whisper "nice
American" and disappear back into the night.

### Origin of Shoulder Insignia (Patches)

During the Civil War the use of special insignia or badges to
denote divisions and corps became widespread. In battle such distinctive markings served a useful purpose in that they assisted in
the assembling of units which had become scattered in combat.
All Civil War Army Corps had distinctive badges which were worn
usually on the hat. They were colored red, white or blue to indicate the first, second or third divisions of the Corps.

The first use of the "patch," according to official sources,[28] is
believed to have been when General Philip Kearny had his men
wear a red diamond on their hats to designate the Third Division,
III Corps, Army of the Potomac. (The scheme of having a *division*
wear the *corps* badge in red, white or blue was prescribed later.)

The Army of the West had no badges until they came into contact with the Army of the Potomac. When one veteran of the XV
Corps saw the stars on the caps of XII Corps soldiers, he registered
his soldierly disapproval by inquiring:

"All you boys generals?"

Asked about his own corps insignia, he slapped his cartridge
box and said it was "Forty rounds in the cartridge box and twenty
in the pocket." Unwittingly he had created a patch for his corps:
a cartridge box with the words "forty rounds." The Thirteenth Infantry, then part of the XV Corps, now features this device in the
crest of its official coat of arms.[29]

[28] *The Soldier's Guide* (Field Manual 21-13, June, 1952), pp. 50-52.
[29] Other Civil War corps badges: I—Disk; II—Trefoil; III—Lozenge;
IV—Triangle; V—Maltese Cross; VI—St. Andrew's Cross; VII—Crescent;
VIII—Star; IX—Shield, crossed by anchor and cannon; X—Square bastion;
XI—Crescent; XII—Star; XIII—none; XIV—Acorn; XV—Cartridge box
("forty rounds"); XVI—Crossed cannon; XVII—Arrow; XVIII—Trefoil
cross; XIX—A Maltese-cross-like figure made by a square with a triangle
at each corner; XX—Star; XXI—None; XXII—Pentagon cross; XXIII—
Shield; XXIV—Heart; XXV—Lozenge on a square. Source: Colonel James
W. Powell (Kansas City: *Customs of the Service*, 1905).

In 1898 a new system of badges was prescribed. Enlisted men continued to wear them on the cap, but officers wore them on the left breast.

But division insignia were not worn on the shoulder until World War I. The Eighty-first Division is credited with being the first to wear a shoulder patch. On their own initiative they sewed cloth wildcats on their arms before going overseas. On arrival in France they were ordered to remove the unauthorized insignia but the division commander protested on the ground that the War Department had not ordered them to do so before leaving the States and had thereby given tacit approval. (The fact was that the division got overseas before the War Department took official cognizance of what was happening.)

GHQ in France decided that it was a pretty good idea after all, countermanded its order and instructed the commanding generals of all other combat divisions in France to create insignia for their units. All units of the American Expeditionary Force were later authorized to select their insignia. In 1920 the War Department established the principle of granting shoulder insignia to all units of division size or higher.

In exceptional cases a unit smaller than a division is authorized to have its own patch.

## MILITARY MASCOTS

"Little magician" is what the word "mascot" originally meant. The affinity between soldiers and animals—particularly dogs—is undoubtedly as old as the profession of arms. Birds, lions, elephants, pigs and ponies are among the many animals which have been adopted as military pets and promoted to mascots.

Fairfax Downey (best known among military men for his *Indian Fighting Army*) has written a boy's book called *Mascots*.[30] He tells the stories of more than forty military mascots from the "Battle Lion of Rameses II" to those of the Korean War.

[30] Fairfax Downey, *Mascots,* illustrated by Augusto Marin (New York: Coward-McCann, Inc., 1954).

## Old Abe and Young Abe

One mascot has been commemorated on a division shoulder patch: the "Screaming Eagle" of the 101st Airborne Division, the heroes of Bastogne in World War II (or "The Bloody Bastards of Bastogne," as they less poetically dubbed themselves).

The Eighth Wisconsin Regiment of the Civil War had a famous eagle mascot known as "Old Abe," named after President Lincoln. "Old Abe" was carried into battle by an "eagle bearer" (shades of the Roman legions!). Chained to a long perch, he was reputed to have been a good combat soldier; he knew when to shriek arrogant defiance at the enemy and when to hit the dirt with his "eagle bearer" when the enemy's shells began drowning him out. He survived the war and lived to be a pampered old veteran.

The 101st Airborne Division acquired a Wisconsin eagle, captured within a few miles of where a Chippewa Indian had caught "Old Abe." With Wisconsin men as "eagle guards," and a master sergeant as "eagle bearer," the twenty-five-pound "Young Abe" was posted between the colors of the 101st Division.

But apparently the modern-day eagles are not of the same feather as their Civil War forebears. "Young Abe" was not trusted to fly loose as "Old Abe" had done. When given a live hen for supper, he preferred to keep her as a pet.

"Young Abe" died of some undiagnosed malady before the division shipped overseas. But his image was with them throughout the war and remains today as the "patch" of the 101st Airborne Division.[31]

## William of the Seventeenth Infantry

During the Korean War, Colonel William ("Buffalo Bill") Quinn invented the Seventeenth Infantry's "Buffalo" nickname, had a white "buffalo statant" added to the blue shield of the regiment's official coat of arms, acquired a live bison named William for the regiment, and almost succeeded in having the animal flown to Korea. (The Air Force was willing, but higher headquarters in

[31] Sources: M. P. T., " 'Old Abe,' War Eagle of the 8th Wisconsin," *Military Collector & Historian*, September, 1952; and Downey, *op. cit.*

"Old Abe"

Japan disapproved on the grounds that "the current situation in Korea precludes the feasibility of care and feeding of the buffalo calf, and that, accordingly, it is not desired that the animal be shipped to this command.")

William was presented to the Seventeenth Infantry in 1951 by Mr. Gene Clark, a rancher in Independence, Kansas, who raises buffaloes. He was two months old and weighed ninety pounds. Congressmen from Kansas joined the regiment in trying to have the animal shipped to Korea. By the time the last request was disapproved in 1953, William weighed a portly but unportable 1,200 pounds! [32]

### Comanche

The following order was published at Fort Riley, Kansas, in about 1876:

The horse known as Comanche, being the only living representative of the bloody tragedy of the Little Big Horn, June 25, 1876, his kind treatment and comfort shall be a matter of special pride and solicitude on the part of every member of the 7th Cavalry to the end that his life be preserved to the utmost limit. Wounded and scarred as he is, his very existence speaks in terms more eloquent than words of the desperate struggle against overwhelming numbers, of the hopeless conflict and the heroic manner in which all went down on that fatal day.

The commanding officer of Troop I will see that a special and comfortable stable is fitted up for him, and he will not be ridden by any person whomsoever, under any circumstances, nor will he be put to any kind of work.

Hereafter, upon all occasions of ceremony (of mounted regimental formation) Comanche, saddled, bridled, draped in mourning, and led by a mounted trooper of Troop I, will be paraded with the regiment.

Comanche had joined the Seventh Cavalry ("The Garry Owens") as a five-year-old in the spring of 1868, and had become the personal mount of Captain Myles W. Keogh. He won his first wound stripe on the Cimarron River, when a Comanche arrow pierced his flank. He was wounded again in 1870 and 1873 in skirmishes with renegade Indians.

---

[32] Sources, Downey, *op. cit.; Army Lineage Book, op. cit.;* correspondence between the author and Colonel Sidney C. Wooten, Commanding Officer, Seventeenth Infantry Regiment in 1954.

After the Custer Massacre, in which Keogh, the colorful ex-soldier of fortune, was among thirteen officers and 212 men killed, Comanche was found near death on the battlefield. His bullet-riddled body was lifted into a government wagon and gently transported away. Troopers of the Seventh Cavalry nursed him back to health. With their own notions on accomplishing "the end that his life be preserved to the utmost limit," they brought him buckets of beer on pay days.

Comanche died in 1891 at the age of 28 and was buried with military honors at Fort Riley, Kansas. His skin was mounted and is now on display in the museum of the University of Kansas at Lawrence.

## REGIMENTAL TRADITIONS

*"Every trifle, every tag or ribbon that tradition may have associated with the former glories of a regiment should be retained, so long as its retention does not interfere with efficiency."* Colonel Clifford Walton, British Army.[33]

A proud regimental tradition is to a military organization what "being from a good family" is to an individual. First, it is a thing you are born with or without; you can't really feel any personal credit for having it, nor any personal chagrin for *not* having it. Second, and much more important, unit or family traditions serve a common purpose of setting a standard to live up to.

In a new country like ours you find less value attached to tradition. We are in the position of a very distinguished Napoleonic marshal whose father was a butcher. During the course of a rather stuffy discussion of genealogy he pointed to his chest and said simply, "I am my own ancestor." Presumably there are many of his relatives today who point with pride to being "descended from a Marshal of France." (Some of them are undoubtedly butchers.)

In our commendable zeal for "democracy" we must not lose sight of the practical, unsentimental value of legitimate tradition. Family pride will not save a degenerate son but it may furnish a wavering individual the tiny impetus he needs to "choose the harder right instead of the easier wrong." Unit pride will not in itself make

[33] Quoted by Lawson, *op. cit.,* on the title pages of both volumes.

heroes out of cowards, but it has often held a wavering battle position during that vital moment when the scales can be tipped to victory or defeat by a hair.

We can't *invent* tradition. But we must not overlook the proud traditions to which we are already heir and which will serve to make a modern soldier want to measure up to his military ancestors at Valley Forge, Gettysburg, the Marne, Bastogne and the Pusan Perimeter.

Several factors militate against the formation of regimental traditions in our Army. First, American soldiers do not write *or* read much about the history of their profession. Second, we have long had a policy of personnel rotation which keeps people from serving long enough with any one unit to learn or appreciate its traditions. The new plan for "unit rotation" ("Operation Gyroscope") should do much to remedy this last situation. Finally, we have a sort of subconscious feeling that a respect for "tradition"—particularly "military tradition"—is alien and, even, vaguely "un-American."

I point these things out only to explain why I am unable to provide several pages of interesting U. S. regimental traditions. They are not available from official Army historical sources. There is no point in digging them out of old military history books. The only legitimate source is the regiments themselves—nothing can really be called a regimental tradition if it is not well known to the men serving in that regiment today.

Here, however, are what you might call "representative" traditions of some American regiments.

### The Old Guard

The Third Infantry, as we have already seen, has the tradition of marching in parades with bayonets fixed. For ceremonies the regiment also turns out the color escort in uniforms of the Revolution. The unique insignia of the "Old Guard" (the knapsack strap) has also been mentioned.

### The Rock of Chickamauga

The Nineteenth Infantry Regiment is commanded by its junior second lieutenant on Organization Day, September 20. This commemorates the day in 1863 when the highest ranking officer left in action was a second lieutenant. The regiment's crest—"a rock charged with the shoulder strap of a second lieutenant of infantry of 1863"—symbolizes the victory on that day which gave the outfit its proud nickname, "The Rock of Chickamauga."

### Garry Owen

Almost a century ago, the Seventh Cavalry Regiment adopted the rollicking drinking song of the Fifth Royal Irish Lancers, "Garry Owen." The origin of this song bears a strange parallel to the origin of West Point's "Benny Havens." "Garryowen" is Gaelic for Owen's Garden, an inn near Limerick, Ireland, which was the favorite haunt of the Fifth Lancers. (Similarly, Benny Havens' Tavern, opened on the West Point reservation in the early 1820's, had been a favorite meeting place of officers and—when Benny's elaborate grapevine told them the coast was clear—of cadets.) "Garry Owen" came into the Seventh Cavalry when a great many ex-troopers of the Irish Fifth Lancers immigrated to the U. S. and joined the Seventh. Custer's favorite, the song signaled the charge with which the Seventh defeated the Cheyennes in the Battle of the Washita in 1868. "Garry Owen" was played the day in 1876 when Custer led the Seventh Cavalry to its fate on the Little Big Horn.

### Bucktails

In the state capitol building at Harrisburg, Pennsylvania, the tail of a buck deer is displayed on the flagstaff of the old Forty-second Pennsylvania Volunteer Regiment. During the Civil War a requirement for joining that regiment had been for a recruit to present the tail of a buck he had shot.

The First Maryland Regiment, CSA (now the 175th Infantry Regiment), was given official authority to display a captured "bucktail" and its color "in commemoration of the gallant conduct in driving back the Pennsylvania Bucktail Rifles" during an engagement near Harrisonburg, Virginia, on June 6, 1862.

The Sixth Infantry Regiment (now the Second Infantry) during the War of 1812 was authorized to wear bucktails on their shakos (hats) in place of the pompons worn by other regiments. This is illustrated in Plate 6 of Kredel and Todd's *Soldiers of the American Army,* 1941.[34]

### The Cottonbalers

The Seventh Infantry ("Cottonbalers") is probably our most distinguished regiment. Unlike the Third Infantry, the Seventh is one of the original units constituted in 1784 that has had the good fortune to participate in all our wars. As a result, the colors of the Seventh Infantry display sixty campaign streamers—more than any other U. S. regiment.

Their nickname and the crest of their coat of arms go back to the cotton bales which were supposedly used in the Battle of New Orleans.[35]

In an army that is notoriously music-less, the Seventh Infantry is distinguished by several regimental songs. "The Girl I Left Behind Me" is their marching song. They have another one known as "Cottonbaler Boys."

But a song composed and originally sung by the Seventh Infantry is a juke-box favorite at the time of this writing:

### "Dogface Soldier"

I wouldn't give a bean to be a fancy-pants Marine,
I'd rather be a dogface soldier like I am:
I wouldn't trade my old OGs [36] for all the Navy's dungarees
For I'm the walking pride of Uncle Sam.
On all the posters that I read it says the Army builds men—
So they're tearing me down to build me over again.

---

[34] From the *Military Collector & Historian,* August, 1949. Editor F. P. Todd's comments on a note submitted by William E. Goodman, Jr.

[35] The following explanation for this misconception was furnished me by my uncle, Major General Haydon L. ("Koje") Boatner, who has done extensive research into the Battle of New Orleans. Old prints and lithographs of the city of New Orleans frequently showed cotton bales as a sort of trademark or identification. When one such "doodle" appeared on an early picture of this battle, the assumption was made that cotton bales had been used as breastworks. Similar "artistic license" has led to misconceptions about Washington's crossing of the Delaware, Custer's Last Stand and the Charge of the Rough Riders at San Juan Hill (which was made on foot, not on horses).

[36] Originally this was "OD's" for "olive drab"; the new uniform color is "olive green" which, fortunately, fits just as well.

I'm just a dogface soldier with a rifle on my shoulder
And I eat a Kraut (Chink) for breakfast every day.
So feed me ammunition, keep me in the 3d Division,
Your dogface soldier boy's okay.[37]

## Most-Decorated Units

The Sixteenth Infantry Regiment is the Army's most decorated. It has been awarded ten Distinguished Unit Citations (one regimental, six battalion and three company DUC), four French Croix de Guerre, one French *fourragère* of the Médaille Militaire, one Belgian *fourragère,* two Belgian Citations in Orders of the Day, and two Meritorious Unit Citations. (*The Army Lineage Book.*)

The Forty-seventh Infantry Regiment is probably the second most decorated. Its decorations are identical in type and number with those of the Sixteenth Infantry, with the following exceptions: the Forty-seventh has a Battalion Croix de Guerre; it has no *fourragère* of the Médaille Militaire; it has only one French Croix de Guerre awarded the entire regiment; and it has only one company Distinguished Unit Citation. (*Op. cit.,* p. 193.)

The Thirtieth Infantry Regiment ("San Francisco's Own") ranks high in the list of "most-decorated units." It has seven DUC, two French Croix de Guerre, one French *fourragère,* and two MUC. (*Op. cit.,* p. 153.)

## The Washington Artillery

A proud and famous military organization is the Washington Artillery of New Orleans. Having fought its guns in every battle of the Civil War, this unit is alleged to be the only one which refused to surrender at the end of the war. Its officers and men buried the guns, burned the caissons and limbers, and rode their battery horses home.[38]

Back in New Orleans they got permission to form the "Washing-

[37] This information on the Seventh Infantry's songs is from correspondence between the author and Colonel Charles E. Johnson, Regimental Commander in 1954. "Dogface Soldier," words and music by Bert Gold and Ken Hart. Copyright, 1942, Shawnee Press, Inc., Delaware Water Gap, Pennsylvania. Used by permission.

[38] The episode bears considerable resemblance to Thomas Nelson Page's classic short story "The Burial of the Guns."

ton Artillery Veterans Charitable & Benevolent Association, Inc."
Then they proceeded to hold secret infantry drills and assemble
weapons. In 1870, when "carpetbag" rule had become too intolerable, they acquired two miniature brass cannon, improvised shrapnel from all sorts of random hardware, and drove Longstreet's
Metropolitan Police off the streets.

In the regular service, the Washington Artillery sent a battery to
fight in Cuba. They distinguished themselves again in World Wars
I and II.

### Message to Garcia

Captain Andrew S. Rowan, whose accomplishment of a mission
in Cuba during the Spanish-American War (1898) was immortal-
ized in Elbert Hubbard's story "A Message to Garcia," had served
with the Nineteenth Infantry ("Rock of Chickamauga") and the
Fifteenth Infantry ("Can Do").

### "America's Foreign Legion"

Several American units have never served within the continental
United States. They include the Thirty-first Infantry Regiment,
which calls itself "America's Foreign Legion"; the Sixty-fifth Infantry Regiment (of Puerto Rico); the Twenty-fourth and the
Twenty-fifth Infantry Divisions. The Twenty-seventh Infantry Regiment ("Wolfhounds") has not served in the U. S. since 1915.

### The Ballad of Roger Young

The 148th Infantry Regiment (Sixth Ohio) was the unit in which
Roger Young won the Medal of Honor during World War II and
inspired "The Ballad of Roger Young."

### Bloody but Unbowed

The 135th Infantry Regiment (First Minnesota) was the unit
that sustained the greatest losses during the Civil War and still kept
fighting.

### ORIGIN OF THE TERM "NATIONAL GUARD"

The National Guard in the United States can trace its name to
the French Revolution. And, in a way, the French are indebted to
the American Revolution for the term. Here is the connection.

During the summer of 1789 the French started their long-brewing revolution by tearing down the Bastille. With the collapse of royal power and authority there arose the need for some force to maintain a semblance of order in the capital. The "National Guard of Paris" was accordingly established and soon imitated throughout the country. The first commander of this organization was the famous and popular Marquis de Lafayette—a man with some previous experience in revolutions!

When Lafayette came back to the United States for a visit in 1824 the Eleventh New York Artillery was turned out to meet him. One of its battalions (later the Seventh New York) happened to have plans for establishing themselves as a separate corps, and they were trying to think up a suitable name for it. While its officers were standing around awaiting the VIP party's arrival, one of them proposed the name "National Guards" in honor of their distinguished visitor. It was adopted.

Volunteer militia in Philadelphia and elsewhere soon appropriated the same name. In 1862 the state of New York adopted the name for *all* its volunteer militia units. In 1903 the term "National Guard"—the "s" having been dropped somewhere along the line—was recommended by Congress for all state militias. Before long it was so used.

# CHAPTER 5

# Soldier Slang and Jargon

## Soldier Lingo

IN a list of U. S. soldier words and expressions you will find a candid picture of the soldier himself.

The first part of this chapter is a basic glossary of current Army talk—words which today's recruit would probably hear during his first few months of service.

The second portion of this chapter consists of words and expressions confined pretty much to the Old Army. I have included them because of a feeling that they deserve preservation in soldier literature, if not in soldier talk.

## PART I: CURRENT SLANG AND JARGON

**Army brat**   Army child. Originally reserved for officer offspring, now applied to *all* Army children. The expression is not considered offensive, but it is best for an "outsider" to smile when using it.

**Asiatic**   Odd in behavior; "goofy." It is applied to a soldier who has "missed too many boats" back to the ZI (*q.v.*).

**"As you were"**   Drill command used to revoke or correct a previous, incorrect command. Commonly used off the drill field to preface a correction.

**"At ease"**   Another drill command that permits soldiers to relax in ranks but requires them to keep the right foot in place and

remain silent. It is used off the drill field as an order for silence
(SR 320–5–1).[1]

**AWOL**   "Absent without leave"; "over the hill" (*q.v.*).

**bad time**   Days absent without leave, in desertion, in the hospital as a result of misconduct, or serving the sentence of a court-
martial. This must be made up by adding the same number of days
to an enlistment.

**BCD**   Bad Conduct Discharge.

**bellyache** (or B-ache)   Alibi or complaint. Used as verb or
noun. Of West Point origin.

**belly robber**   Mess Sergeant (now called Mess Steward).

**bird colonel**   Full colonel (whose insignia is an eagle ["bird"]).
Sometimes called "eagle colonel," from which term "bird colonel"
probably evolved. Arose from necessity to distinguish from lieutenant colonel, who is often called a "light colonel" (from abbrevia-
tion "Lt. Col.").

**blitz**   Shine; "buck" (*q.v.*). Term is from a commercial metal-
polishing rag with trade name "Blitz cloth." *Blitz* is German for
"lightning," whence *blitzkrieg* ("lightning war"). ("Blitz cloth" is
undoubtedly so named because it is supposed to work "as fast as
lightning".)

**bolo**   A "bolo" is a man who fails to "qualify" (i.e., get the
minimum score) on the range with his weapon. Since this is the
ultimate disgrace to a soldier, "bolo" also means an "eight ball."
It is used also as a verb ("to bolo"). The word is Spanish for the
short, heavy chopping knife which the Filipinos used for agricul-
ture and also for war. (A "machete" is the same type of weapon.)
The slang word comes from the feeling that a man who couldn't
use a firearm should be given a bolo in its place. Colby [2] tells the
classic Army story about the sergeant who watched a recruit miss

[1] Army Special Regulation 320–5–1, *Dictionary of United States Army
Terms,* November, 1953, referred to hereafter simply as "SR."
[2] Colonel Elbridge Colby, *Army Talk,* Princeton, 1942. See main bibliography for comment on this standard military book. Hereafter cited as
"Colby."

the target four times in a row. Finally, in exasperation, the sergeant shouted the command, "Fix bayonet! Charge!"

**bone** To strive; to work or study hard. A "file boner" is "bucking for promotion" (*q.v.*). "Bone a reverse" is West Point slang for getting on somebody's "black list."

**BOQ** Bachelor Officers' Quarters. "Bedlam" was used many years ago.

**brass** Senior officers. From "brass hats," the World War I expression for staff officers and senior commanders because of the heavy gold ornamentation which these officers wore on their cap visors in foreign armies. Originally a derogatory term, like "GI" it has been so commonly used by journalists that it has lost its stigma. Again, however, "When you say that, smile." The word is also used in an entirely different sense to mean empty cartridge cases. ("Sergeant, get a detail to police up the brass from the firing line.")

**break** Short rest period (which "breaks" the march, instruction, or other duty). Soldiers customarily get a "ten-minute break" in every hour; it is usually announced by "Take ten." The "coffee break" has become a national institution among office workers.

**buck** A versatile and much used word. It means "responsibility" in such expressions as "passing the buck." The latter, apparently, is what is meant by "the old Army game" (sheer slander, by the way). A "buck slip" is the routing form by which papers are "circulated" for comment, action, approval, etc. The word means to "oppose or fight" ("don't buck the system"). It means to "shine" or "improve in appearance" or "strive" when used in such contexts as "buck your shoes and brass," "buck up your squad leaders," and "bucking for sergeant." A "buck private" is the lowest category of private (i.e., lower than a Private First Class). In this latter sense, the expressions "buck sergeant" and, recently, "buck general" (i.e., brigadier general) are used.

**bug out** Retreat in panic and disorder (Korean War origin). Implies a greater degree of panic than to "how able" (*q.v.*).

**bulldozer** Now associated primarily with a piece of engineer equipment, this purely American word has an interesting derivation.

It has been traced to Louisiana where the "bulldozer" was a whip made from an item which delicacy forbids my mentioning. (The Mexicans still make this type of whip or quirt.) Negroes were "bulldozed" into voting the Democratic ticket. (Within the last week I have heard an ancient Louisiana Negro use the word "bull-dooze" in the original colloquial sense of "to coerce.") The term has also been used to signify "pistol whipping." (A nonmilitary note: The Southerner has ceased to use the "bulldozer" politically since he has completed the emancipation of the Negro from slavery and reduced the Republican population to an insignificant number.)

**bunk fatigue** Bed rest, "sack time," "horizontal engineering," etc.

**bust** Demote. Probably a literal translation from the French *casser* and the Dutch *kasseeren* (both meaning "to break"). "Cashier," incidentally, comes from the Dutch word, and has nothing to do with the financial type of cashier who would "pay off" an officer before his dismissal from the Service. In one of Bill Mauldin's classic cartoons of World War II, Willie is saying to Joe: "I got seniority. I got busted a week before you did." The word "bust" is also used by soldiers in the sense of a "blowout" (celebration) as in "beer bust."

**butt** Remains of anything. ("I have three weeks and a butt to go on this hitch" [*q.v.*]).

**butterfly** To philander. Japanese pidgin English. A Nipponese "girl san" will assure her current boy friend that she is faithful and does not "butterfly" on him.

**chicken** Unreasonably insistent on observance of military minutiae; "GI" (*q.v.*).

**chicken colonel** Same as "bird colonel" (*q.v.*).

**chow** Army food.

**CG** Commanding General. Formerly known also as "Kay-O."

**chopper** Helicopter (also "whirley bird").

**circulation** The mass of papers and other "literature" which is "circulated" through the various "desks" of a military office or headquarters. Not quite the same as "distribution," which is defined as "an official delivery of anything, such as orders or supplies" (SR). After orders had arrived "through distribution" they would become part of the "circulation" in a headquarters.

**cit** Civilian

**cits** or **civvies** Civilian clothes. (Journalists favor the word "mufti"—see Chapter 3 for origin—which soldiers rarely use.)

**CKC** Khaki (from official designation "cloth, khaki, cotton").

**CO** Commanding Officer ("the Old Man" [*q.v.*]).

**Commo** Communications Officer (from abbrevation "Comm. O."). The often heard "Commo officer" is redundant, as is "PIO officer" (for Public Information Officer). "Commo" also is used for "communications" in such expressions as "commo wire" and "communications trench" (a trench for protecting *personnel,* not *signal wire,* along routes between exposed positions).

**dai jobu** Japanese. Used by Americans to mean "O.K." Actually, this is a considerable corruption of the term's precise meaning of "all right" only in certain specific cases. (If, for example, you drop your watch but do not break it, the watch is *dai jobu.*)

**DD** Dishonorable discharge.

**deadline** Keep a vehicle in the shop for repairs.

**detail** An official word, most commonly used to mean a small group of men assigned to a specific task which is usually of a temporary nature ("guard detail," KP detail, police detail, "sump hole" [garbage pit] detail). Another purely official sense of the word is a "temporary shift of a commissioned officer to another arm or service without effecting a change in his basic branch" (SR). ("He put in a detail with the IG [Inspector General's Office] right after the war.")

**dog tag** Identification tag issued to soldiers and worn on a chain around the neck. (See Chapter 4 for origin.)

**dog face** Soldier. Not considered particularly derogatory.

**dog robber** Officer's orderly; "striker." Mathews [3] quotes *Har-*

---

[3] Mathews, *op. cit.,* bibliography at end of Chapter 3.

*per's Magazine* in 1868 in which "dog robbers" are defined as "the cooks and detailed soldiers who were the occupants of the second table ["last serving"?] of an officer's mess." Presumably, a soldier who had to wait on the officers was considered by his buddies to be so low as to be forced to steal his food from scraps thrown to the dogs. Derivations of "orderly" and "batman" are in Chapter 3.

**doughboy**   Infantryman. Dates from the Civil War. In 1887, the following explanation was printed: "A 'doughboy' is a small round doughnut served to sailors. . . . Early in the Civil War the term was applied to the large globular brass buttons on the infantry uniform, from which it passed, by a natural transition to the infantrymen themselves." [4] This seems to be the most plausible origin. Mathews also gives space to the theory that "doughboy" "may have arisen from [the word] adobe applied quite early by Spaniards in the Southwest to army personnel" (presumably because much of their duty consisted of making " 'dobe" for the construction of their forts and barracks in the desert). Some currency has been given to the unlikely theory that infantrymen were called "doughboys" because the flour which they used as a substitute for "pipeclay" to whiten their uniforms turned to dough when it rained.

**dry run**   Practice. See also "jawbone."

**extend**   Voluntarily remain in Service or on a tour of overseas duty longer than originally called for.

**eyewash**   Measures taken to make something "look good" for inspection or other occasions. There is an implication of deceit. Closely associated with "whitewash," it is not quite the same thing. "Eyewash" is practiced to prevent defects from being noticed; "whitewash" is what you do to cover up the transgressions of a subordinate to attempt to keep him from being held strictly to account for them. The latter term is not confined to the soldier's vocabulary.

**"Fall out"**   A drill command which permits soldiers to leave ranks but requires that they remain in the immediate vicinity, prepared to "fall back in." Colloquially, the expression means to relax

---

[4] Quoted in Mathews, *op. cit.* Radford, *op. cit.,* generally agrees. The American Navy got the term "doughboy" from the British Navy.

when associating in an off-duty status with one's military superiors. Due to the camaraderie which characterizes relationships among true soldiers, there is more social mingling among subordinates and superiors in military life than in civilian life. Official distinctions of rank, rigidly observed when there is work to be done, are relaxed when "off duty." A new officer, fresh from civilian working conditions in which he saw The Boss only during working hours or at an occasional "office party," finds the off-duty social mingling of the Army confusing. He has to learn how to "fall out" when talking to a military superior in the club. An old soldier knows when and how much to "fall out" around officers.

**field** A soldier performs his duty "in the field" or "in garrison." Even soldiers who vastly prefer the "coffee cooling" life in garrison will go to great pains to get "in the field" on occasions (usually during good weather) so as to avoid the stigma of not being known as a good "field soldier." The same psychology motivates staff officers (no matter how competent) to "get out with the troops in the field" and avoid the odor of being known as "strictly a staff officer."

**file** An individual ("He's a sloppy file"); also, one number on a promotion list ("You are fifty-seven files ahead of me on the list of captains.") (See also Chapter 3.)

**file boner** One who strives for professional advancement ("to gain files").

**flap** An emergency, "crisis," "storm," or confused situation. "The staff was in a flap getting ready to brief the General." The type of commander who keeps his subordinates in an uproar over relatively insignificant matters is known as a "flap maker." The word probably was borrowed from the British staff officer in World War II; it became a much used word in the American officer's vocabulary during the Korean "flap."

**fogy** (also fogey) A pay increase awarded automatically (every two years) for military service. A *Congressional Record* of 1879 uses the terms "fogy ration, or longevity ration" in the sense we employ "fogy" today. (Mathews)

**footlocker** Small trunk, so called because it is usually kept at the foot of a soldier's bunk in barracks.

**foxhole** A rather picturesque word, now part of the national vocabulary. It is a small pit from which one or two men can fight while having some protection from enemy fire. A "slit trench" is a similar species of "hasty field fortification" which differs in that it is a "prone shelter" (the length and breadth of a man, but only about two feet deep).

**fruit salad** Ribbons worn above the left pocket to represent decorations and awards.

**gangplank fever** Psychotic tendencies developed by reluctant warriors about the time they are scheduled to ship overseas.

**GI** (*noun*) Disparaging term for soldier. (See page 149 for usage notes.)
    (*noun*) Gastro-intestinal upset ("He had the GI's.").
    (*adj.*) "Government Issue" or "galvanized iron" (as in "GI can."
    (*adj.*) "Strictly by the book." ("The new lieutenant is really GI—he makes us salute and everything.")
    (*verb*) To prepare something for inspection by scrubbing with soap and water. ("Friday night we'll GI the barracks for Saturday inspection." This would be a "GI party.")

**gig** To report a delinquency (to "skin"). Of West Point origin —where the word is used only as a verb or adjective—it was picked up in Officer Candidate Schools and civilian military schools where it was corrupted into a noun. ("I will give you a gig.")

**goldbrick** To loaf, or a loafer. Of civilian origin.

**go-to-hell cap** A "garrison" or visorless cap, also known as an "overseas" cap. Name probably derives from the "breezy" or "go to hell" look of Air Corps (*sic*) pilots to whom this cap was originally issued. The billed item of headgear is known as the "service cap."

**guardhouse lawyer** An eight ball who thinks he knows all the tricks of circumventing military law and regulations. Probably so called because he and his "clients" spend so much time in the guardhouse as a result of his "counsel."

**hash marks**   Service stripes (diagonal stripes worn on the left sleeve of an enlisted man's coat or shirt to indicate the number of three-year enlistments he has served). Instituted in 1782 in our Army, the word probably comes from the French *hachure*, which in English means "a short line used in drawing and engraving" (Webster) and also to bring out relief on maps.

**"He's had it"**   Picked up from the British to mean "finished" or "out of luck." Highly flexible, the expression can mean that the man is dead or that he missed the last bus back to camp.

**high-ball**   Hand salute (railroad origin).

**hitch**   An enlistment. (Mauldin's Willie to Joe: "I'm going to need a long rest after this war. I think I'll put in a hitch in the Regulars.") The word probably originates from the idea that soldiers are "hitched" to the Service.

**honcho**   "Boss" or "supervisor." Korean War slang.

**housewife**   A sewing kit. The word has been adopted as official nomenclature (SR and T/O&Es).

**how able**   To pull out of a position or location in a hurry. Implies a lesser degree of panic than "bugging out" (*q.v.*). "How able" is old phonetic alphabet for "H.A.," meaning to "haul" something unprintable.

**ichi ban**   Japanese, meaning literally "Number 1," hence "of prime quality." The Chinese equivalent is "ding how."

**jawbone**   Credit; also range firing or taking an examination not "for record." Synonym: "dry run." It also means "temporary," as in "jawbone promotion." In the pre-Pearl Harbor Army, soldiers got "canteen checks" or Post Exchange credit coupons and paid for them at the end of the month. ("Jawbone payday" was the day they were issued. The amount you could draw in these "pontoon nickels" was in accordance with enlisted rank to keep men from getting too far in debt. One of the Old Army rackets was for certain capitalists to buy "canteen checks" at *below* par value from men needing cash before the end of the month. Then they would also sell the "chits" on credit at *above* par prices to men who had used up all their own canteen checks and who wanted to get things from the PX.) The origin of the word is not known, but it might be interesting to do a little speculating. "Jawbone" is an obsolete word for "a minstrel song," castanets and a jew's-harp. (Mathews) Obviously we can rule out these meanings. Colby says that, although some authorities consider the word of recent vintage, it has been traced (in the sense of "credit") to the *London Times* in 1862 and to the British Army whence it may have come from the Canadians. He says it was used among cattlemen in the Northwest in the 1880's. It may come from an Oriental word used for "credit" among merchants in the Philippines and sounding like "jawbone." But I think Colby is closest to the probable origin when he points out that it combines the American slang of "bone" for dollar with the idea of talking or "jawing" a man into extending you credit.

**jeep**   A quarter-ton truck. From the "GP" ("general purpose") in the vehicle's official nomenclature. The amphibious vehicle known as the "Duck" got its name from the official designation "DUKW."

**jockstrap outfit**   A unit which places much emphasis on athletic achievement.

**KP**   Kitchen police (soldiers detailed by roster for work as "cooks' helpers"). DRO's (dining-room orderlies) are no longer used since soldiers now eat "chow-line style" rather than "family style" (in which food was put on the tables and kept replenished by DRO's).

**line**   Military duty is divided into two general types: "line" and "staff." A line outfit is one that would serve "in the (battle) line"; such expressions as "line officer" and "line duty" are associated with units "of the line."

**long johns**   "Long-handled drawers," or long underwear.

**macht nichts**   German, "It doesn't matter."

**Maggie's drawers**   The red flag waved by the pit detail to indicate that a soldier firing on the range has missed the target altogether. The expression may possibly be associated with what the

British Army calls a "magpie," a black and white flag to signal a shot in the "outermost division but one of the target." (Radford)

**make**  To promote. Originates from the official wording of the "make list" which is usually to the effect that "The following named men are made corporals [for example]." Used also as a noun: "a new make." Of course the soldier also uses the word in the more conventional slang senses.

**max**  Derived from "maximum," and meaning maximum score or grade ("I got a cold max on the last exam"). If a girl were referred to as a "max" it would mean that she scored 100% in pulchritude.

**medic (medico)**  A medical man.

**NCO**  Noncommissioned officer (i.e., corporal, or sergeant).

**ninety-day wonder**  Derogatory term for OCS graduate.

**OCS**  Officer Candidate School.

**OD**  Officer of the Day (in the Navy, "OOD").

**Old Man**  The commanding officer, regardless of age, of any unit of company or higher level.

**outfit**  A military organization ("What outfit you in, Buddy?").

**over the hill**  Absent without leave (AWOL). As a matter of interest, the British call this "French leave" and the French call it "English leave" (*filer à l'anglaise*).

**panic button**  When a "crisis" appears to be impending, you "push the panic button." The expression is confined to military staffs where "panics" are more frequent than in line units.

**police**  Our Army uses this word to mean "clean up" and "make orderly." A "police detail" is one which picks up trash, not law-breakers. Years ago each unit had a man detailed as "Provost" or "police sergeant"; despite what you might expect, this man was concerned with cleanliness and sanitation, not orderly conduct. (Powell) If you are thrown off a horse you have been "policed."

**poop**  Information of any sort, usually written (on a "poop sheet"). Of West Point origin, probably from fact that the cadet adjutant makes important announcements in the mess hall from a balcony known as the "poop deck" (from its resemblance to a ship's poop deck).

**possible**   To "shoot a possible" is to get the highest possible score (i.e., all "bulls") in a series of shots on the firing range.

**PX**   Post Exchange (formerly the "canteen").

**QM**   Quartermaster.

**red leg**   An artilleryman. (A feature of the Old Army dress uniform for officers was a stripe down the leg in their branch color; Artillery officers wore a red stripe.)

**red-line**   To indicate by drawing a red line through a soldier's name on the pay roll that he has not been paid. ("I got red-lined last month because I was on furlough payday.")

**re-up**   Re-enlist.

**RHIP**   "Rank hath its privileges." (See page 139.)

**sack**   Bed, "the pad," "hay," etc. Originates from "bed sack." ("Sack in," "hit the sack," "sack rat [or artist]," "clock some sack time," etc.)

**service-school service stripe**   A "V" created when the vertical seam of the khaki trousers is let out to accommodate an expanding posterior.

**shack**   A versatile word which now has to do with the immoral relationship between a soldier and a member of the opposite sex. Probably from Hawaii, the Philippines and Panama where soldiers would visit their girl friends in native shacks.

**shavetail**   Originally an Army mule (Mathews cites an example of this use in 1846). Applied to newly commissioned officers as early as 1899 (Mathews). Term originates from fact that newly purchased Army mules arrived with shaved tales. Resemblance between conduct of new mules and new officers is apparent.

**short-timer**   One whose enlistment or tour of overseas duty has almost expired.

**SI** Saturday inspection. Confined to West Pointers. Since cadets save their best uniforms for the rigid Saturday inspection, they would use such expressions as "SI trousers" to mean their best trousers.

**side arms** Old Army mess-hall lingo for cream and sugar. ("Pass the side arms, please.") Literally, side arms are the weapons worn in the belt ("at the side"), such as pistols, swords and bayonets.

**six-by** A truck having a six-wheel drive.

**skin** Same as "gig" (*q.v.*) in meaning and usage.

**skoshee** Japanese *sukoshi,* "a little," "a few," "some." (See "toksan," below, for pronunciation note.)

**SNAFU** "Situation normal, all fouled up."

**SOS** Creamed beef on toast ("slop on a shingle"). In official language it stands for the "Services of Supply."

**stockade** Officially, "a confinement facility, usually of temporary construction" (SR). Soldiers use the word to mean the "guardhouse."

**striker** An officer's orderly, "dog robber" (*q.v.*).

**TO&E** "Tables of Organization and Equipment" (T/O & E). These are the official instructions on how a unit is to be organized (with respect to the number of personnel and their grades), and what equipment they are authorized to have.

**toksan** Japanese *takusan,* "much" or "many." (Pronounced "tok-san"; the Japanese do not sound the "u".) The word is generally used by soldiers with Far East experience.

**yard bird** Recruit, or the lowest grade of private. Now used more in the sense of "eight ball" or "one who acts like a recruit." Origin unknown. Colby suspects it may come from "area bird" (a West Point cadet who spends much time "walking the area" for excess demerits). Possibly of penitentiary origin.

**ZI** "Zone of the Interior," meaning the United States, in the case of the American Army.

## PART II: OLD ARMY LINGO

**awkward squad**   Extra instruction, held after duty hours for men who need special attention in close-order drill.

**beaucoup**   French, "much" or "many." This word was current during and after World War I. It was revived during World War II.

**bedlam**   Bachelor officers' quarters (BOQ).

**beno**   (Rare except at West Point.) This is an announcement that a scheduled formation has been cancelled. Originates from "there will *be no* parade this afternoon." Prior to announcement, Cadets will have been shouting "Let's have a beno."

**bubble dancing**   Dishwashing (also "pearl diving").

**bugle**   To stall for time. Of West Point origin (and little used except by cadets), the word goes back to the days when the end of a class was signaled by a bugle call. A cadet who was improperly prepared in his lesson would try to stall off recitation and be "saved by the bugle."

**cabbage**   "Folding money" (paper currency).

**choggie**   As a verb, it means "to climb a hill," or to carry a load up a hill. As a noun, it means a native bearer (used in Korea to carry supplies). Of Korean War origin.

**chop-chop**   Used by old China hands to mean "hurry." In Japan it is pidgin English for "food" or "eat."

**cinch**   Unforgivable breach of mess-hall etiquette, "cinching" consists of taking the last or next to last piece of food from a platter without holding it up for the DRO (dining-room orderly) to replenish. Good for a fight in the Old Army.

**coffee cooling**   Loafing, deadbeating, goldbricking. Presumably it originates from the custom of prolonging a coffee break on the pretext that the coffee is too hot to drink immediately. Of ancient vintage.

**cold**   Absolutely without error or qualification, as "cold sober," "cold max" (i.e., 100%).

**cold jug** (or **cold bottle, fish**)    A person without humor, who appears to get no joy out of living.

**cool** (*verb*)    To set back or knock out ("He got cooled with a rock").

    (*adj.*)    Complete ("I spent a cool 100 bucks on pass").

**copacetic**    Russian, "O.K." (roughly).

**crawl**    To admonish, bawl out, "chew."

**dingbat**    A headquarters clerk.

**Fire Call**    A confused situation or formation. "All fouled up like Fire Call."

**fish eyes**    Tapioca.

**flanker**    Tall man (because he is usually placed on the flanks of a unit during ceremonies).

**footlocker cocktail**    A drink concocted by certain desperate soldiers from toilet preparations (after-shave lotion, etc.) and liquid shoe polish (by straining through bread).

**foot sloggers**    Infantrymen.

**gat**    Slang for revolver. Probably from Gatling gun, the machine gun invented by Dr. R. J. Gatling and first used in the Civil War. (Not soldier slang but of military origin.)

**goat**    West Point slang for a man near the bottom of his class academically. A "hive," one near the top of the class, is known as an "engineer" from the fact that only a small number of vacancies exist each year in the Corps of Engineers and the top graduates traditionally select that branch in peacetime. The "class goat" is the one who graduates at the bottom ("anchor man" at Annapolis).

**Gook**    Originally "Island" slang for the lowest class of natives. Applied to the North Koreans at the beginning of the Korean War as a term of contempt. Later carelessly applied to any Asiatic natives.

**gravel agitators** (**crushers**)    Infantrymen.

**hooch**    Liquor. Interesting in that this common item of civilian slang was brought into the language by soldiers who encountered it when we took over Alaska (Colby).

**hop**  A dance. Most commonly used at West Point. A "boodle hop" is one at which refreshments are served.

**hump**  In the Old Army, a man was "over the hump" when he had completed half of his service. Another type of "hump" occurs when you have ahead of you on the promotion list an exceptionally large number of men of about the same age and grade (who have to be promoted before you yourself can be advanced). "Humps" in promotion lists occur after wars when a large number of officers are retained in the Service; officers who enter the Service after the war are "behind the hump."

**IC**  "Inspected and Condemned." Formerly stamped on Government property no longer serviceable.

**"the Islands"**  Originally this meant only the Philippines. If a man were speaking of the Hawaiian Islands he would not refer to them as "the Islands."

**jerk a belt**  To relieve a soldier for improper performance of duty. If a soldier were sleeping on guard it was the custom to remove his belt before waking him up so as to have evidence that he was actually asleep.

**John**  A recruit. A "second John" was a shavetail (*q.v.*).

**Johnson bar detail**  Back before the days of electric floor buffing machines, the floors were waxed by men armed with Johnson bars.

**JOP**  "Junior officer present."

**Manchu Law**  An old regulation requiring officers to return to troop duty after being absent four years on other types of assignment.

**meat wagon**  Ambulance.

**muck**  Muscle ("bone muck": to develop oneself physically).

**mule skinner**  Man who works with mules. Of civilian origin. Presumably, such men are tough enough to skin a mule alive.

**pearl diver**  The KP who washes dishes.

**pebble pushers**  Infantry; sometimes refers to runts (short men) who, allegedly, have to push their way through the pebbles.

**pipe** To look at or to anticipate with great interest or expectation ("Pipe the blonde." "He's piping leave.").

**Podunk** A home town or home-town newspaper. "Podunck" was "a small place between Hartford and Windsor" in 1666. The word is also suspected to be of Indian origin and meaning "a neck or corner of land." (Mathews)

**pontoon nickels** Post Exchange (canteen) chits. Possibly originates from the fact that you could get them on credit and they would "hold you up" (financially) until pay day.

**rice bill** Money spent supporting an Oriental "shack job" (woman)—in Hawaii, the Philippines or Panama.

**runt** Short man.

**salt-water stripes** Temporary rank. Term originates from fact that acting NCO's usually have to be made on troop ships.

**section eight** An obsolete administrative means of eliminating soldiers who were substandard. (The officer equivalent was "Class B.") Soldiers are now eliminated for "inaptitude," "unsuitability" or unfitness under the provisions of newer regulations. However, old soldiers still use such expressions as "He's 'section eight' material."

**shortstop** To help yourself to food being passed to somebody else at the table who asked for it. (Usually good for a fight in the Old Army.)

**skag** A cigarette.

**slum** Meat stew. A West Point football song is named "Sons of Slum and Gravy." A "slum burner" is a soldier (as a "hay burner" is a horse or mule) or, sometimes, an Army cook. "Slum" was once the mainstay of the Army diet; the word has gone out with the advent of more luxurious rations.

**sunshiner** One who has served too long in the tropics (i.e., been out in the hot sun too much). It is also applied to people who have gotten so used to tropical duty that they complain of weather that is even mildly cold (Colby).

**tailor-mades** "Store bought" cigarettes, as opposed to "Bull Durhams" or "roll-your-owns." The Old Army soldier had to economize by "rolling his own."

**tin school**   A civilian military school. This term, while not con-
noting any serious disapprobation, probably comes from the expression "tin soldiers" (i.e., make-believe or toy soldiers).

**trooper**   Formerly a cavalryman (the cavalry was organized
into "troops" rather than batteries [artillery] or companies [all
others]). Now the term is applied to paratroopers—although the old
"parachutists" are not particularly fond of it.

**twenty-per-cent man**   Old Army loan sharks. "GI interest" was,
"I'll give you $4 now and you give me back $5 on pay day."

**WPPA**   "West Point Protective Association," a mythological
organization which has never existed either in the flesh or in spirit.

# CHAPTER 6

# Significant Dates in the Forming of U. S. Military Tradition [1]

1636    October 7—182d Infantry Regiment and 101st Engineer Battalion, both of the Massachusetts National Guard, are the oldest existing American military organizations. Distinction owed to unbroken lineage from North and East Regiments, respectively, which were organized on this date from Colonial "train bands." (See page 66.)

1638    March 17—Boston's Ancient and Honorable Artillery Company chartered; not actually organized until June. (See page 67.)

1652    The Army's second oldest regiment, the 176th Infantry Regiment (First Virginia—"The Old First") of the Virginia National Guard, organized in the Colony of Virginia as the Charles City–Henrico Counties Regiment of Militia.

1756    September 8—First pitched battle fought by Americans on the soil of what is now the U.S. was won against French regulars at Lake George, N.Y. (Montross, *op. cit.*)

1775    June 14—U. S. Army founded when Congress authorized enlistments of companies of riflemen to serve the United Colonies one year.

---

[1] Precise dates are difficult to fix. Even when records are available, there can be much bickering over technicalities. Unless otherwise stated in parentheses, dates in this chapter are from the official *Army Almanac* (hereafter cited as AA), or from the Office, Chief of Military History, Department of the Army (cited as OCMH).

June 14—Infantry established.

June 16—Engineers, Quartermaster, Adjutant General and Finance established. (OCMH dates; AA assigns date of March 16, 1802, to establishment of Corps of Engineers.)

July 21—Artillery established (OCMH).

July 27—Medical Corps established. (Medical "Department" established 1818.)

July 29—Chaplains established.

November 10—Marine Corps founded. Made permanent in 1798.

December 13—American Navy born when Continental Congress authorized building thirteen war ships.

1776    January 2—First American flag, bearing seven red and six white stripes, raised at Cambridge, Mass.

January 6—Battery D, Fifth Field Artillery Battalion, constituted as Alexander Hamilton's Provincial Company of Artillery of the Colony of New York. This is the oldest organization of the *Regular Army*.

January 14—Re-enlistment furloughs initiated by General Washington. The policy has continued.

December 12—Cavalry established. (Known since 1950 as Armor.)

1777    January 5—Mines first used in America; powder kegs floated on Delaware River to destroy British ships.

June 14—Flag of thirteen stars and thirteen stripes adopted.

December 13—Inspector General Department established. Baron von Steuben is the first IG.

1778    February 25—Gambling in the Army prohibited by orders.

June 28—"Molly Pitcher" (Mary Ludwig Hays) at the Battle of Monmouth.

October 30—Army numbered 595 men.

1782    August 7—Purple Heart decoration established.

1783    November 3—Continental Army disbanded except for one infantry regiment and two artillery battalions.

1784    June 2—Army disbanded by Congress as being "inconsistent with the principles of republican government." An eighty-man caretaking establishment was retained to guard supplies.

June 3—Militia units ordered by Congress to be formed to protect northwest frontiers.

Third Infantry Regiment ("The Old Guard") constituted as First American Regiment, the oldest *regiment* in the *Regular Army*.

1787   September 29—Army of 700 men authorized.

October 3—Indian trouble in the West led Congress to authorize stationing 700 troops for protection of settlers. This was important step toward establishing Regular Army.

1789   September 29—Regular Army established when Congress passed an act to recognize and adapt to the Constitution the military organization already in existence.

1790   April 30—First general organization of the Army under the Constitution provided for one regiment of infantry (three battalions composed of four companies each).

1791   March 3—First Infantry Regiment constituted. It is the second oldest regiment in the R. A., since it was originally designated "Second Infantry Regiment." (See Chapter 4.)

1792   December 27—The Legion of the United States, consisting of four sublegions, was announced by Congress as having been established by the President.

1794   November 13—Whisky Rebellion broken up by Army troops.

1796   November 4—U. S. agrees to pay Tripoli $83,000 a year for protection of American commerce against Barbary pirates.

1802   March 16—United States Military Academy founded at West Point, N.Y.

1808   April 12—Second and Fifth Infantry Regiments constituted.

1811   December 24—Enlistment bounty authorized as 160 acres of land, $16 and three months' extra pay on discharge.

**1812**  May 14—Ordnance Department established.

June 26—Army reorganization. All infantry regiments to have ten companies. Entire Regular Army to consist of twenty-five infantry regiments, four artillery regiments, two dragoon (mounted infantry) regiments, one regiment of riflemen, and engineer troops.

**1813**  June 1—"Don't give up the ship!" were the dying words of Captain James Lawrence during the engagement of his frigate *Chesapeake* with H.M.S. *Shannon* off Boston.

**1814**  August 24—British burned White House and Capitol to avenge the American burning of York (Canada). Only eight Americans died in defense of national capital.

**1821**  March 27—Blue prescribed as color for Army uniforms.

**1824**  First service school of the Regular Army was established at Fortress Monroe, Virginia, as The School for Artillery Practice.

**1832**  June 11—Eagle adopted as insignia of rank of colonel.

**1833**  March 2—First Constabular Squadron (First Cavalry) constituted as the Regiment of Dragoons. This is the Army's oldest cavalry unit.

**1836**  March 6—Alamo falls to Mexicans after two-week fight in which all 187 American defenders were killed. The force, commanded by Col. W. B. Travis, included James Bowie and Davy Crockett.

**1846**  May 19—Third Armored Cavalry Regiment (Light) constituted.

**1855**  August 15—Army cap replaced by a black felt cap with black feather ornaments: three feathers for field officers, two for company officers (captains and lieutenants) and one for enlisted men.

**1856**  January 31—Sixth Infantry established at Fort Clay, Nebraska, to protect pioneers in prairie country.

**1860**  June 21—Signal Corps established (OCMH date; March 3, 1863 has also been given). Our Army is the first to have such a corps of officers and men whose exclusive duty is communications. During the Navaho campaign, on this same date, the Army is supposed to have used Morse Code visual signaling for the first time in combat (AA date).

1861   January 16—Fourth Infantry Regiment established at Fort Chehalis, Washington, to protect settlers.
August 5—Flogging in the Army abolished by Congress.

1862   January 30—*Monitor* launched, ending era of wooden warships.
March 8—Army ordered formed into four corps by President, without consulting the General in Chief.

1864   February 29—Grade of Lieutenant General (three stars) revived.

1866   September 30—Regular Army strength at 38,540.

1876   June 25—Custer and 212 men of the Seventh Cavalry ("Garry Owen") massacred at Little Big Horn, S.D. The horse "Comanche" was the only survivor.

1877   Army went without pay for seven months because Congress failed to make appropriations.

1879   May 9—Eighteenth Infantry Regiment established at Ft. Assiniboine, Washington, as defense against Indians.

1890   December 29—End of Indian Wars of the United States with Army victory at Wounded Knee Creek, S.D.

1898   April 27—"Triangular" concept of military organization initiated when Army establishes regiments of three battalions each.
July 18—Transportation Division established in QMGO. (OCHM date). On July 31, 1942, this became the Transportation Corps.
October 7—Khaki cloth formally adopted for U. S. Army uniforms.

1902   June 30—Olive drab color adopted for uniforms.

**1903**  August 16—First Army Chief of Staff, Lieutenant General Samuel B. M. Young, took office.

**1907**  December 23—Signal Corps issues specifications and calls for bids for an airplane that would fly for one hour, carry two passengers, and make forty mph. (Wright brothers had invented airplane in 1903.)

**1909**  July 30—First airplane accepted by War Department. Final test flight had been at Fort Myer, Virginia, by Orville Wright and Lieutenant B. D. Fulois. Plane was built to military specifications by the Wright brothers for $25,000. They received a $5,000 bonus for delivering a faster plane than specified.

**1915**  January 1—Panama Canal opened; built by Army Engineers.

**1917**  October 23—First American artillery shot fired in World War I, by Battery C, Sixth Field Artillery, in the Lunéville sector.

**1918**  June 28—Chemical Warfare Service established.
July 30—Joyce Kilmer killed in action. As a sergeant of the 165th Infantry, Forty-second ("Rainbow") Division, he was on patrol beyond the Ourcq River in France.
September 26—History's greatest single mass troop operation launched. For forty-seven days, in the Meuse-Argonne offensive, more than 1,200,000 Americans pushed forward on a ninety-mile front.
November 4—The 332d Infantry (Regiment), only American unit to fight with the Italian Army on that front, crossed the Tagliamento River.

**1920**  February 23—Chief of Staff given rank of General.

**1926**  December 31—"Rolling" type of collar on service coat replaced "choker" type worn during World War I. Design remained a single-breasted sack coat, but with a notch lapel collar.

**1938**  January 7—Spiral khaki leggings replaced by canvas leggings.

January 23—Entire battalion airborne for first time in America.

**1940** July 18—Test parachute platoon organized.

September 16—Selective Service Act signed. First time in U.S. history that citizens universally liable for military service in peacetime.

September 26—Military Police established.

**1941** December 7—Pearl Harbor attacked by Japanese.

**1942** March 13—Dogs first inducted officially into U. S. Army.

May 14—Women's Army Corps established (as WAAC).

July 31—Transportation Corps established ("The Transportation Division, QMGO," was established July 18, 1898.)

**1945** May 8—VE Day. Germans signed unconditional surrender.

August 6—First combat atomic bomb dropped on Hiroshima, Japan. (The first test bomb had been exploded July 16 at Alamogordo, N.M.)

August 14—VJ Day. Japan surrenders. (Formal surrender, Sept. 2.)

**1950** June 25—North Korean Communists invade South Korea.

July 4—American patrols from Task Force Smith make first enemy ground contact with Communists north of Osan.

**1953** July 27—Korean fighting ends. (Armistice signed July 26.)

**1954** January 21—First atomic submarine, *Nautilus*, launched. The keel had been laid June 14, 1952, at Groton, Connecticut. She went to sea under her own power January 17, 1955.

**1957** October 1—"Army Green," as a color for uniforms, will begin to replace olive drab and officers' "pinks and greens."

# CHAPTER 7

# "Customs of the Service"

"CUSTOMS of the Service" have been called "the unwritten law of the Army." Just as English "common law" has become incorporated into the written law, so have many of these customs been written into Army regulations. The distinction between *official* and *social* customs of the service is admittedly arbitrary—and there is overlapping. However, the intent is to distinguish between those customs which govern "official" relationships and those which apply to "social" or "off-duty" relationships.

Customs of the Service are changing constantly to keep up with new social and technological trends in the country and in the Army. The old taboos against an officer's carrying bundles or pushing a baby carriage do not make much sense in these days of no servants and a rising birth rate.

There is nothing sacred about a military custom any more than there is anything hallowed about a rule of grammar. Both must keep pace with the times.

We should, however, know and understand the accepted practices before advocating innovations. Winston Churchill was well aware of the grammarian's prejudice against ending sentences with a preposition before he announced that this is "a form of arrant pedantry up with which I will not put."

It would not do for an officer to decide that there was nothing wrong with pushing a baby carriage and then undertake to wheel one through the corridors of the Pentagon just to demonstrate his independence of thought. But if on a party night the car's on the blink and little Bosco must be transported to the post nursery, an officer should by all means slap him in the perambulator and get rolling.

Some out-of-date customs are hung onto for sentimental reasons. Others serve as a historical link with the past; their observance adds color and interest to the military profession. Some "efficiency expert" who didn't understand what makes soldiers tick might propose that the West Point cadet uniform be eliminated in favor of something more "practical" and better suited to mass production by the garment industry. You could propose doing away with the Retreat Gun on the pretext of saving ammunition and man-hours. Regimental colors could be eliminated on the grounds that they are old-fashioned and no longer serve any "practical" purpose. We could stop playing Taps at military funerals and abolish military bands so that more men will be available for KP and drill.

As a matter of fact, the Army's bands *were* drastically reduced after World War II but it was not long before this "penny wisdom" was recognized as "pound foolishness"; even the efficiency experts had to give in to the clamor from soldiers and civilians to "bring back the bands."

The veteran soldier does not need to be "sold" on the importance of tradition and customs. But he occasionally re-examines them and does away with ones that no longer serve any purpose or that interfere with military efficiency. But before we condemn a custom we owe our predecessors the courtesy of realizing that the custom once made sense. We must be sure our refusal to accept a custom is not based on poor judgment or ignorance.

Older armies have accumulated fascinating customs and traditions throughout the years. Several British regiments, for example, do not stand and drink when the king is toasted. They are "above suspicion." In some past action they so distinguished themselves that the king excused them from the symbolic proof of loyalty represented by drinking to his health. The Royal Navy toasts the king without standing. The story is that the Prince of Wales, while visiting a warship, cracked his head on a low beam when the toast was proposed. "When I'm king there'll be no such foolishness," he announced. And, when he succeeded his father, the Royal Navy held him to the promise.

It was the custom years ago in some American regiments for key staff officers to tender their resignations when a new colonel took command. The new colonel would, of course, refuse to accept the resignations, thereby indicating that he had full confidence in the staff he had inherited.

A senior officer in approaching a junior with a message used to preface it with, "Major Patton presents his compliments to Captain Walker and says ————." A junior, on the other hand, could not "present his compliments" to a senior. (This conformed to prevalent civilian etiquette of this period.)

An old practice that could well be revived is the "by your leave" of the junior when overtaking a senior on the street or passing him on a stair.

At some military funerals you will still see a horse following the casket with officer's boots reversed in the stirrups.

But let's pass now to those customs and courtesies that are still very much in effect.

## PART I: "OFFICIAL" CUSTOMS OF THE SERVICE

### The Desire of the Commander

The "wish" or the "desire" of a commander is generally assumed to have the same weight as an order. Military law backs this idea to the extent that a person can be convicted for failing to obey an order even though that "order" was expressed in the form, "I would like you to do so and so."

Notice that we said the wish has the same weight as an "order." Nobody can be convicted of failure to disobey an "illegal" order. It requires little imagination to see the absurd things that could happen if this custom were taken too literally.

### Familiarity with Subordinates

It is improper for an officer to get familiar or "personal" with an enlisted man. The same applies generally in official dealings with officers junior to him.

Since regulations and customs forbid a military man's being familiar with his military superiors, it is only common decency that the senior should govern his own conduct accordingly.

This custom is not snobbery but is dictated by sound psychological principles that have been periodically challenged and proved time and again to be valid. Familiarity *does* breed contempt. A green second lieutenant has enough of a problem winning the respect of his men without complicating it with the conditions bred by familiarity. As an officer becomes more competent he can afford to be less formal with his men because they will respect him for his demonstrated ability. It would probably surprise many civilians to know that there is a higher degree of camaraderie between the officers and men of elite units than there is in recruit outfits. This was particularly noticeable in the German Army of World War II; officers and men of elite units, who were "all business" during combat, had achieved a degree of mutual professional respect that permitted them to relax many of the barriers between ranks when off duty.

## RHIP (Rank Hath Its Privileges)

In the Army as in every other form of human relationship it is recognized that the heavier load of work and responsibilities imposed on higher commanders deserves recompense in the form of higher pay and extra privileges. For this reason officers do not perform fatigue duty and are provided better living accommodations, rest facilities, etc.

No reasonable man resents the existence of these privileges of rank so long as they are not flaunted or abused.

"RHIP" exists in more extreme forms in civilian life than it does in the Army; but, for some reason, the "civilian mind" finds it harder to accept in the military service. For this reason the officer must go out of his way to avoid any unseemly exhibition of his privileges.

Rank also has its obligations—not the least of which is to see that one's subordinates' rights are respected and that they get the privileges they deserve.

## Official Knock

One rap on the door is considered to be the "official knock" and is the warning for persons in that room to be ready for an official visit.

This practice is observed at West Point, for example. Tactical Officers on inspection tours use the "official knock." A Plebe who has been ordered to report to an upperclassmen in his room would rap more than once.

The custom is useful in garrison when noncoms occupy separate rooms. The "official knock" might well be used by a battalion commander entering a company commander's office, while men of the company coming into the same office would knock twice.

(The jokers in the unit will, of course, amuse themselves by "unintentionally" using the official knock and throwing the unsuspecting occupants of a room into a frenzy. These humorists should be dealt with in the same manner as those addicted to shouting "Attention" in a quiet squad room.)

### Officers Not Called to Attention

It is not proper for officers to observe the enlisted men's custom of calling attention at the approach of a senior officer. The question then is how to get officers to attention without shouting the command. If assembled in a conference room or a theater awaiting the arrival of a senior officer the problem is handled this way in many commands. Somebody is posted to watch for the arrival of the senior officer. As he sees the latter approach he may sound off "At ease, gentlemen" as a warning. When the senior enters the room, one officer will announce "Gentlemen, the Commanding Officer." All officers stand at attention until told to be seated.

### Fatigue

Officers or noncoms should not normally perform fatigue duty. While this is a "privilege" of rank, it stems from the assumption that officers and noncoms will be kept busy *planning* and *supervising* fatigue details.

### No Excuses

This is one of the most firmly established concepts of military service. It is one which the recruit finds hardest to accept.

Like most other customs, this one is firmly rooted in sound psychology. A military man must succeed in any assignment or job he gets. It is assumed that he will not resort to illegal means but aside from that the only important thing is whether he accomplishes the mission or not. In event of failure the assumption is usually that he lacked the necessary aptitude or did not try hard enough. The answer is, "No excuse, sir."

Many "impossible" tasks have been successfully accomplished because a man knew he would not be able to excuse a failure. If a commander were to practice a policy of allowing subordinates to alibi their way out of failures you can imagine what would happen to the efficiency of his command.

There will be times when a commander will want to know the *reason* for a failure. If a subordinate should see fit to *volunteer* reasons he must be sure they are valid and not simply excuses with which he hopes to exonerate himself. As a rule it's best to remain silent even at the expense of suffering a minor injustice.

A military leader must remember that his subordinates also are brought up in the tradition of "no excuses." He must not be taken in by the slick talker who can justify all his failures; he must not assume that the man who takes his medicine is doing so only because he has nothing to say in his own defense.

### No Thanks

It is an ancient and almost forgotten military custom that you don't thank a superior when he does something for you in the course of his official duties. For example, you should not thank the commanding officer for approving your leave request. When a soldier receives his pay, he does not thank the paying officer for it. A company commander would not thank the inspecting officer for giving his company a favorable report.

In purely social relationships—as opposed to the official ones just cited—the normal "civilian" courtesies, of course, apply. The point is that official relationships are supposed to be *above* considerations of "personal feelings" (favoritism or hostility); thanking a superior for an official action could imply that he was showing you favoritism.

Obviously there will be times when the rhetorical use of "Thank you, sir" cannot be avoided without appearing rude or arrogant.

If a senior officer were to conclude an inspection by saying, "Captain, I want to compliment you on the splendid appearance of your company," the captain is expected to say something. A soldierly answer would be, "General, I will inform the men."

### Use of the Third Person

Officers should never use the third person in speaking to a superior. In former days it was the custom for the First Sergeant, for example, to say to his company commander, "Sir, would the Captain care to do so and so?" This practice crept into the officer corps during World War II, possibly because of the large number of noncoms who were commissioned and could not break themselves of the habit.

Until fairly recent years it was *prescribed* that "Officers should require that enlisted men when addressing them use the third person, as 'Will the Captain,' etc., not 'Will you,' etc. . . ." [1] This practice has fallen into disuse. Although many old soldiers still use the third person in addressing officers, this is a custom we can let die a natural death.

### Use of "Sir"

A soldier in addressing a military superior uses the word "Sir" in generally the same manner as does a well-bred civilian in speaking to a person to whom he wishes to show respect. In the military service, however, the matter of who says "Sir" to whom is clearly defined; in civilian life it is largely a matter of discretion.

The proper, natural and graceful use of "Sir" is something that comes only with training and experience in the Army. Some officers (and men) fall into the habit easily; others must work at it.

As a *general* rule "Sir" is used in speaking either officially or socially to any senior. The word is repeated with each complete statement. "Yes" or "No" should not be used in speaking to a superior without including "Sir."

On the other hand, "Sir" should not be said with every other breath to the point of obsequiousness. In official dealings between officers who know each other well it is proper to use the word with less frequency.

A military man should be careful about the use of "Sir" in conversations with civilians. A too frequent "Sir" with civilians may be embarrassing to them and smack of "bootlicking."

---

[1] Colonel James W. Powell, *Customs of the Service* (Kansas City, 1905).

In speaking with a general officer you should use the word "General" in the place of "Sir" wherever this can be gracefully done. For example: "Good evening, General," rather than "Good evening, sir."

I have a personal prejudice against the use of "Sir" by ladies in speaking to officers. Certainly any reasonably young woman could gracefully use "Sir" in addressing any general officer or a gray-haired full colonel. But I feel that the use of "Sir" by ladies to any officer below the rank of colonel should be done on the basis of age rather than the insignia on his shoulder. Army wives, by the same token, hate to be called "Ma'am" by a junior officer, unless the latter is young enough to be her son!

### By Direction of the President

Only "by direction of the President" can an officer be required to serve as a subordinate to an officer whom he ranks. This is in line with the time-tested military principle that seniority must be respected.

Like all policies, there will be many instances when assignment on the basis strictly of seniority will work to the detriment of military efficiency. As a policy, however, the observance of seniority is unassailable. It is another safeguard against favoritism and politics creeping into military affairs.

Needless to say, the President is not personally consulted every time command of a company is given to a lieutenant who is three days junior to one of the platoon leaders in that company. The authority is delegated. But the orders assigning any officer to a position of command over an officer senior to him will include the phrase "by direction of the President."

### A Buck for the First Salute

For years it has been traditional for a newly commissioned officer to give a dollar to the first man who salutes him. Many an old soldier has cashed in on his knowledge of this tradition by posting himself strategically near a graduation ceremony of an Officer Candidate School and picking up several fast bucks.

A dollar for the first salute.

### Mixing Items of Civilian Apparel with Uniforms

A military man when in uniform should never have any item of civilian clothing visible. He may have on a pair of polka-dotted shorts or red suspenders. But he should not wear civilian socks, gloves or belts that are not of the proper military design, color, and material.

He should never have a tie clip, key chain or civilian belt buckle visible. Collar stays should be of the "invisible" type. Handkerchiefs should be OD or plain white.

It is never correct for an officer to mix items of uniform with civilian clothes—even for athletics. You should never see an officer downtown or in the PX wearing an old pair of "pink" trousers with a sports jacket, for example (although this is common among veterans and their relatives). It would not be proper for him to show up at the golf course in fatigue trousers or an OD shirt. On the other hand, there could hardly be any objection to exercising in the gym or doing a little road work on the country trails in a mixture of civilian and military (fatigue) clothing.

### "Officer and Gentleman"

Much democratic mirth has been inspired by the military tradition that an officer is expected to be a gentleman. In early armies, military leadership—like civilian leadership—was a monopoly of the nobility or "gentlemen." Now that officer rank is bestowed on the basis of merit, officers are still expected to "act like gentlemen."

Those addicted to guffawing over the phrase "officer by act of Congress" should have pointed out to them that this is an *obligation* rather than a modern-day "patent of nobility." In military law, for example, an officer can be court-martialed for "ungentlemanly conduct," whereas an enlisted man cannot.

### "The Colonel's Lady and Judy O'Grady..."

Back in less democratic days it was customary to distinguish between the "wives" of soldiers and the "ladies" of officers. Obviously, this is unacceptable in a day when we use "lady" to mean any adult human who is not a male. (For example, we see the term "charlady," rather than "charwoman"; a streetwalker is now a *"lady* of the evening.")

### Personal Services of Enlisted Men

Soldiers may be detailed as "strikers" to perform certain "house-keeping" tasks for officers, particularly in the field. When a unit moves into a bivouac area, for example, the officers will be involved with supervisory tasks which do not leave them much time to arrange sleeping accommodations and dig in.

In most other armies, officers have a soldier who is assigned as a personal servant. Called a "batman" in the British service, he is sort of a military valet. This idea is, of course, offensive to Americans. But we should realize that an officer's talents will be much more profitably used if he can be spared certain menial chores. This service is completely logical and inoffensive if not abused.

No enlisted man should be assigned to perform the duties of personal orderly if he feels this duty is degrading. There are plenty of men in any unit who are glad to get this type of work. They may be razzed at first by their buddies for being "dog robbers" but this is usually good-natured. If the orderly performs his duties in addition to regular military jobs, it is customary for the officer to pay him for his services. The commanding officer should be asked to prescribe the amount and see that it is uniform throughout the unit.

There is nothing improper about having enlisted men perform other personal services for officers and their families provided that they don't interfere with the soldier's performance of duty, are completely voluntary, and involve no use of government time or materials. These "personal services" would include such things as painting, carpentry, the repair of radios, etc. Needless to say, it is customary to pay soldiers for such services.

### Some "Customs" the Army Can Do Without

The Army is an extraordinary organization in the literal sense of the word. It is not surprising, then, that it has developed some peculiar customs. In the Army we make a fetish of sanitation, personal neatness, punctuality, honor, immaculate police of grounds and living quarters, obedience to orders and the absolute authority of the commander.

But we have developed a few other customs—frequently referred to sneeringly as "the old Army game"—that a conscientious officer may not be able to eliminate single-handed but which he should not be guilty of perpetuating.

"Passing the buck" is, perhaps, the most outstanding of these. Proper and skillful delegation of duties is the mark of the successful commander. "Passing the buck," something entirely different, is attempting to pass your own work or responsibility onto another (usually junior to you).

"Rank-pulling" is not only proper but expected in official matters. That's why military leaders have rank. The senior officer present in any military business is totally responsible for everything that happens. In the Old Army, promotion was extremely slow and considerations of who ranked whom reached into all aspects of the Army's life. But the tremendous expansion of the service and the influx of "nonprofessionals" has created a situation that has called for re-evaluation of the former exaggerated emphasis on rank even in social matters.

It used to be that an officer could be "ranked out" of quarters by any new arrival on the post who was senior. The victim could then compound the injustice by "ranking out" somebody else. Conceivably the arrival of one senior officer could result in making every family on that post move and would throw the junior officer off the post entirely. This ridiculous practice was perpetuated for many generations, apparently in a spirit of "every dog has his day."

A few enlightened commanders, who themselves had perhaps suffered under the old system, have seen fit to do away with the practice and it is now rare for an officer to be evicted from quarters in which he is settled.

The true leader knows instinctively—or through experience—when it is not proper for him to "pull his rank." He would not, for example, take his place in a chow line or a ticket line ahead of everybody junior to him. In an unofficial discussion he would not use his rank to silence opposition to his own ideas.

A general rule is this: it is proper to use rank in official matters or in social matters only when the interests of the Service are involved (such as settling or, better, preventing a disorder).

"The tail wagging the dog" is a form of improper rank-pulling. It refers primarily to the selfish custom in some headquarters of using the name of the commander to rob subordinate units of equipment or outstanding personnel.

## Other Taboos

"Going over the head of a superior" is like the child's trick of asking Father for something when Mother has already said no.

Servility, "bootlicking" and "apple-polishing" are quickly detected and condemned.

Criticism of superiors in the presence of their subordinates is unsoldierly. Military men do not criticize the President in public. An officer does not make derogatory comments about another officer in the presence of that officer's subordinates. It is considered to be bad taste to discuss a lady's virtue—or, rather, her lack thereof —in the presence of gentlemen. Soldiers should not criticize the Service in the presence of "outsiders."

Gambling with subordinates as well as lending or borrowing money is taboo for obvious reasons.

Offensive language and "filthy stories" are considered out of place in the presence of superiors or subordinates.

Sitting on another soldier's bunk without permission is the mark of a recruit or a man who is trying to start a fight. (The reason is that a soldier's bunk is supposed to stay unwrinkled and ready for inspection during the day.)

Accepting gifts from military subordinates or from civilians with whom one deals officially is forbidden by regulations as well as custom. This is a sensible rule, designed to eliminate personal influences in official dealings. Also prohibited is the shallow subterfuge of presenting gifts to an officer's wife or family.

## Service Semantics

All professions have certain speech peculiarities. Nobody could masquerade long as a sailor if he used such expressions as latrine or bathroom (for "head"), downstairs (for "below") or floor (for "deck").

Army lingo has a few peculiarities of its own. Soldiers are not "boys," "guys" or "fellows," in official language. They are "men" or "soldiers."

The use of "GI" to mean "soldier" was originally an expression of belittlement or contempt. It meant something that was "Government issue" and, therefore, totally devoid of any individuality, intelligence or character. When the Old Army used the expression it was a case of "When you call me that, smile." The expression is closely associated, also, with "GI can" (standing for "galvanized iron"). The GI can, in turn, is associated with garbage. The term gained great currency during World War II and started out as a good-humored expression of self-deprecation by the citizen-soldier. The press picked it up as an apt term for men who considered themselves to be "civilians in uniform" more than soldiers. (Any newspaperman will tell you how much easier it is to fit "GI" into a headline than it is to handle a longer word like "soldier." The word "brass"—meaning, presumably, anybody above the rank of Second Lieutenant—was popular with the press for much the same mechanical reasons.)

You will hear the uninitiated speak of the flag's being at "half-mast" when there is no "mast" any closer to the post than the nearest naval installation. The Army normally flies flags from a staff. The proper expression is "half-staff." "Half-mast" is Navy lingo.

"Shrapnel" is improperly used to mean "shell fragments" these days. There is much to be said in favor of appropriating the convenient word "shrapnel" for another meaning—particularly since true shrapnel is no longer used in our Army. Maybe you consider this to be "a form of arrant pedantry up with which you will not put." But you, like Winston Churchill, should base your decision on taste rather than ignorance of the true meaning of "shrapnel."

"Pants are worn only by women and midshipmen; men wear trousers." This is an old squad-room prejudice and some Old Soldiers still shun the word "pants."

"Rookie" is another word the Old Soldier dislikes. "You have rookies on baseball teams and police forces; in the Army they're 'recruits.' "

A sergeant should not be addressed as "Sarge" except by his personal friends.

### Good-Conduct Medal Worn by Officers

The title of this section will split military readers into two wildly hostile camps. They will read the next paragraphs only to see whether I agree with them; their minds are made up and nothing anybody else says will change them. (So I will be very circumspect.)

For the benefit of others, however, here is what the controversy is about. The Good-Conduct Medal is awarded for excellent behavior, efficiency and faithfulness during a prescribed period of time. It is given only to enlisted men; you can assume an officer is up to these standards or he would be cashiered.

However, an officer has reason to be proud of having been an enlisted man and "coming up from the ranks." This can be the only explanation for an officer's wearing a Good-Conduct Medal. Certainly he does not need to "prove" that his conduct was good.

### Officers' Messes

Unfortunately, there is not much to be said about the customs and traditions of officers' messes in the American Army. We do have officers' *clubs,* but we do not have any permanent officers' messes in the British sense of the term.

In the British Army, the officers' mess is an institution. It is "home" for the unmarried officer, "club" for all officers, and the center of social life at the military installation where it is located. British officers will tell you that The Mess is where the standards and ideals of their service are passed on from the older to the younger officers. The institution is particularly valuable during wartime expansion when the army commissions young men who have more of a gap to bridge between their civilian backgrounds and the standards they are expected to achieve as officers and gentlemen.

The tradition of the British officers' mess would appear to run counter to American social ideas. Actually, there is a need for such an institution in our own Army. It would be the solution to many of our own problems in indoctrinating young officers. The trouble is that you don't "create" a tradition. American commanders have frequently established true officers' messes and run them very successfully—particularly in line units during wartime. But with our rapid turnover in commanders, the mess which one officer creates after months of hard work can be destroyed by a successor who thinks it is not worth the trouble.

## SOME MILITARY MISCONCEPTIONS

### Medal of Honor Holders Rating a Salute

The myth sprang up somewhere along the line that enlisted men holding the Medal of Honor are entitled to a salute from officers. This has no basis in fact.

Although it is customary for the junior to initiate the exchange of salutes, it is completely proper for a superior to salute first. It is possible that after some commanding officer saluted a Medal of Honor holder the word got around that this was expected of all other officers of the command.

### "Fine Him a Buck and Give Him a Carton of Cigarettes"

Another bit of guardhouse lore is that the guard who shoots and kills an escaping prisoner is fined a dollar and given (in compensation) a carton of weeds. This is, of course, sheer garbage—but it's amazing how many men think there's something to the story.

Actually, any guard who shoots a prisoner will be tried "for his own protection." This is no mere formality. The purpose is to find out whether the death of the prisoner was justified—whether the guard used good judgment. The rights of the victim will be defended by the trial counsel and the latter will make every proper effort to prove murder or, at least, manslaughter. But presumably the guard would not have been issued live ammunition unless he were expected to use it if necessary to keep his prisoner from escaping. He will have to prove that the shooting was justified. If the sentinel can prove he was exercising good judgment in the execution of his duty he can be sure of acquittal.

But he won't be fined a dollar. Nor will he be given a carton of cigarettes.

### Sentinel Never Surrendering His Weapon

Although this question has been debated around the barracks stoves since General Kreuger was a corporal, the answer can be found "in the book."

*Field Manual 26–5* (*Interior Guard*) says this: "A sentry quits his piece only on the order of a person from whom he lawfully receives orders while on post. Even those persons should not order a sentry to quit his piece, for inspection or any other purpose, unless an emergency exists."

There it is.

### Manner of Wearing the World War II Occupation Ribbon

The idea got started somehow that you wear the World War II Occupation Ribbon one way if you served in Europe and the other way if in the Pacific. (The ribbon consists of a red and black band in the middle with a white stripe on each end of the ribbon.) It is always worn with the red band to your left, no matter where you served to earn it. A good way to remember this is to keep in mind that when the medal is hanging on its ribbon the red can be only to the wearer's left.

### AIR FORCE CUSTOMS

Most Air Force customs, being of Army origin, are identical with Army customs. There are a few, however, particularly those connected with air travel, that are "original."

*Order of boarding aircraft* is as follows: pilot, copilot, other crew members and then passengers in order of rank. Note that this differs from the Army protocol which calls for vehicles and small boats to be entered in inverse order of rank; it conforms with the naval custom of permitting the senior officer to board a ship first.

*Order of leaving aircraft* is for passengers to leave in order of rank in the case of V.I.P. flights. In routine flights, officers seated near the hatch will debark first, and so on to those who are seated farthest forward.

*Civilian dependents or EM accompanied by dependents* will be loaded after V.I.P.'s and before officers, and will leave in the same sequence.

*Choice of seat* in the plane goes to the senior passenger. In either transport or tactical aircraft the senior officers generally ride as far forward as possible.

*Final authority on the operation of any plane* is the assigned first pilot. All passengers, regardless of rank, are subject to his orders.

*Aircraft carrying general or flag officers* will usually be marked with a detachable metal plate carrying stars appropriate to the highest rank aboard. Such officers will be greeted on arrival by the Base Commander. Other planes are usually met by the Airdrome Officer, who is appointed for one day only and acts as the Base Commander's representative.

*"Waltzing mice"* is an expression some pilots apply to passengers who are unreasonably active while the plane is airborne. Any moving around makes unnecessary work for the pilot while flying on instruments.

*Other airplane etiquette* includes punctuality; observance of safety regulations with respect, particularly, to smoking and the use of parachutes and seat belts. Keep out of the pilot's compartment unless invited to enter. Army personnel who seek transportation on training or navigation flights must realize that they travel at the pilot's convenience. He cannot deviate from his approved flight plan to accommodate a passenger. The pilot must sometimes decide to cancel a flight due to bad weather and you must not question his decision—even if you should be inclined to be so foolhardy.

## NAVAL CUSTOMS

Since a landlubber is likely to spend some time aboard ship, it is important that he know something about certain Naval customs beforehand.

*Coming aboard ship,* officers usually take the starboard (right, facing bow) gangway. When reaching the head of the gangway you face toward the colors and salute. The colors are normally flown from the stern of the ship; if no colors are visible, salute in the direction of the ship's stern. You then turn and salute the Officer of the Deck (OOD), who will normally be standing at the head of the gangway to receive you. This officer, incidentally, will return both salutes. The business of two salutes from the head of the gangway can be a little awkward to the unitiated landlubber and requires agility. But take your time; the sailors will probably be impressed by the fact that you "have the word" and respect their customs.

"Request permission to come aboard, Sir" is the proper thing to say as you salute the OOD. He will probably answer "Permission granted, Sir."

*Leaving the ship* calls for an exact reversal of the procedure. At the head of the gangway you should face the OOD, salute and state, "Sir, with your permission I will leave the ship," or "Sir, I request permission to leave the ship." He will probably say, "It was a pleasure to have you aboard, Sir," to which you should reply in kind ("It was a pleasure to have been aboard, Sir"). Your last act before going down the gangway is to salute the colors.

*The "Bridge"* is the ship's "Command Post" when under way. You should not attempt to go up there unless invited. The ship's executive officer will usually grant you permission to visit.

*Passenger officers should call on the captain.* If there are a large number of officers aboard, they should pick a committee to call on the ship's captain to pay their respects. Arrangements as to time should be made through the executive officer.

*President of the wardroom mess* is the ship's executive officer. At dinner and supper, officers are not seated until the mess president arrives. If for some reason you have to leave the mess early, ask permission from the head of your table.

*Do not overtake a senior* unless in an emergency. If you must pass, naval customs call for you to salute and say, "By your leave, sir."

*Salute the ship's captain* whenever you meet him. Other rules for saluting in the Navy are similar to those in the Army except that naval custom calls for the officer initiating the salute to accompany it with "Good morning, Sir," or other appropriate greeting. (This is also good practice in the Army but is not so generally observed.) When two boats pass each other the senior officer in each salutes the other without rising. The salute is never rendered by naval persons when uncovered—even in reporting to a senior officer or to the president of a military court.

*The cigar mess* was formerly known by the more virile term of "Wine Mess." The ship's counterpart of the Post Exchange is the Ship's Store.

*Do not tip the stewards* who serve you meals and perform duties of orderly in your room. This is their assigned duty.

*Don't whistle aboard ship.* This tradition is observed to eliminate the possibility of confusion with the "bos'n's pipe." (There is much the same tradition in the "city room" of a newspaper where whistling might be distracting to others.)

*Smoking is not permitted* on certain parts of the ship and under certain conditions. It is prohibited on the quarter-deck, for example. Find out the local rules from one of the ship's officers.[2]

## PART II: "SOCIAL" CUSTOMS OF THE SERVICE

Since the beginning of World War II and the resulting expansion of the Army, social customs of the service have been in a state of change. When an officer reports to a new assignment or when a civilian visits an Army post, he should ask about the local "ground rules." In all cases, the local commander will prescribe the degree to which the old social customs will be observed.

The following run-down on social customs of the service should be useful in showing what to expect. It should also assist local commanders and their adjutants in establishing local practices.

### Use of Titles

In writing to military people you use their full titles. In talking to them, however, Army, Air Force and Marine Corps personnel are addressed as follows:

| | |
|---|---|
| All general officers | "General" |
| Colonels and Lieutenant Colonels | "Colonel" |
| Majors and Captains are addressed by their titles. | |
| All Chaplains (regardless of military rank) | "Chaplain" |
| Warrant Officers and West Point Cadets | "Mister" |
| All Sergeants | "Sergeant" |
| Corporals | "Corporal" |
| Privates and Privates First Class | "Private So-and-so" |
| Nurses are addressed by rank. | |
| Specialists, whether first, second or third class are addressed as | "Specialist So-and-so." |

[2] Most of the information on Air Force and Naval Customs is from *The Armed Forces Officer* (Washington, D. C.: Government Printing Office, 1950).

In introducing a military man who is not in uniform, you should mention his service. For example, "Colonel Blitz, *of the Army.*" Since a naval "captain" is equivalent in rank to a full colonel of the other services, he should always be introduced as "Captain Bilge [for example], *of the Navy.*"

An old custom, not generally observed, is to continue addressing an officer socially by the title of a higher military rank he may have held. After a war, for example, when many temporary generals are reduced back to the grade of colonel, they may still be addressed socially by friends as "General."

### Calls ("Courtesy Visits")

An Army Regulation on "Visits of Courtesy" (signed by General John J. Pershing) has just been superseded after remaining unchanged for thirty-four years. While the new AR (632-110) still lets the local commander prescribe how closely he will adhere to "the principles outlined in these regulations," it is obvious that a revival of pre-World War II social customs is afoot.

"Official calls" are of two types. For the sake of explanation, let me refer to them here as "office calls" and "house calls." Within forty-eight hours of his arrival, a newly assigned officer is expected to make two "office calls." These are made to his own immediate superior and to that officer's immediate superior; in military terms, the two officers immediately above him in the chain of command. (For example, a newly assigned company commander would visit his battalion commander and then his regimental commander.)

The second type of call is what we will tag the "house call." The newly assigned officer and his wife will repeat his "office calls" (see above) by visiting the same two officers *in their quarters* "as soon as practicable." The local adjutant will inform him of the calling hours. Custom has for years dictated that these calls be limited to fifteen minutes; the new AR makes this specific.

The above rules apply not only to the newly assigned officer but also to an officer who is visiting for more than twenty-four hours.

Now, how about calls on the other officers of the post? The new officer and his wife wait for a "welcoming courtesy visit" (the official term) from each officer of the post. They return calls within ten days.

On the subject of *farewell* visits the new AR prescribes only that an officer check with the adjutant to find out the local practice.

Within recent years it has been the practice on large military installations to hold a monthly reception in the Officers' Club as a substitute for the individual calls we have been discussing. New arrivals, as well as departing officers and their wives, pass through a reception line.

On many posts it is still customary for all officers to call on their commanding officer on New Year's Day.

*Calling cards* are left when making formal calls. Distribution is as follows. A man leaves one card for each adult member of the household (including guests). Ladies should leave one card for each adult female of the household. As a rule, no more than three of any one card should be left, regardless of the size of the household.

If a bachelor calls on a lady guest it is proper for him to leave cards for the guest's host and hostess, whether or not he knows them.

If you are caught without cards it is considered proper to write your name on the cards of another guest who is making the call with you. You may also make a correction of rank on your cards (in ink).

There is a rather elaborate etiquette of "card leaving" which you can bone up on if you feel it necessary, but the above rules should suffice. Some people are thrown into a tizzy at the prospect of having to leave cards—the mechanical, physical procedure of getting them out of your possession and into the possession of the host. Collect the prescribed number of cards and palm them before you ring the doorbell. If nobody is at home, slide them under the door and be gone—you get "constructive credit" for the visit. If a servant answers the door, announce yourself (after recovering from the shock) and hand him the cards. In other cases try to locate an appropriate receptacle for your cards and deposit them in as natural a way as possible. There is no need to be covert; the host is not trying to "catch you in the act" and hand your cards back, or count them to see whether you have left the proper number.

*Form of calling cards.* Regulations have recently stated that, although the size and style of calling cards are optional, "the most commonly accepted size is 3¼ by 1½ inches, with shaded Roman engraving." The card will show your grade. Branch (i.e., Infantry, Armor, Artillery, etc.) may be shown but is not required. Now here is something new: "service" will be shown only as "United States Army"; it is no longer proper to use the designations "National Guard" (NG) or "Organized Reserve Corps" (ORC). (Appendix C explains the terms "branch," "service," and "component.")

An officer's rank can appear on the same line as his name: "Captain George Shaw Wilson"; or it can be shown in the lower right-hand corner above the line "United States Army."

With the above peculiarities, military visiting cards conform to civilian usage. The full name is usually spelled out; but you can use initials if your middle name is inconveniently long or if you'd just as soon not have it known. Cards should be engraved and ornate lettering should be avoided. Emily Post says that men's cards can be between 2⅞ and 3¼ inches long; between 1¼ and 1⅝ inches wide for "plate-marked" cards. Subtract ¼ inch from these dimensions to get the socially accepted "tolerances" for non-plate-marked cards. Mrs. Post does comment that the plate-marked cards are considered "a little effeminate for a man." [3]

*Formal calls* are those made in the discharge of a social obligation. Strict etiquette prescribes that you be punctilious, and that you restrict the call to fifteen minutes.[4] In case of death in the family of a friend or acquaintance, leave cards at the home. On a small post when one's friends have house guests it is desirable and proper to call on them. Bachelor officers should call upon young unmarried women visiting their friends and pay them such courtesies as asking them to dances, movies, etc. On leaving a post or civilian community, an officer calls on the commanding officer and his other friends. In such cases he should mark his cards "p.p.c." (*pour prendre congé:* "to take leave") in small letters. When obliged to

---

[3] Emily Post, *Etiquette* (New York: Funk & Wagnalls, 1947).

[4] While it is prescribed in the American Army that uniforms be worn for formal calls, the British Army has precisely the opposite practice. "Remember these are social calls. . . . Never pay a call in uniform." Group Captain A. H. Stradling, *Customs of the Services* (Aldershot, England, 1949), p. 68.

leave hurriedly he should mail these cards to his friends and also place one on the bulletin board of the Officers' Club.

*Calling hours* for posts in the United States are 7:30 P.M. to 9 P.M. Sunday afternoon calling hours are from 3 P.M. to 5:30 P.M. In civilian communities, calls are usually made between 4 P.M. and 6 P.M. so as not to conflict with evening engagements.

Remember, however, that there are no hard and fast rules about calling. You must be sure to find out the local ground rules— civilian and military.

*Social functions* form an important part of military life just as they do in civil life. Officers are expected to attend garrison functions and to contribute toward making them pleasant affairs. It is customary for officers to make a point of speaking to the senior officers present and to dance or chat with their wives. It's also a smart policy to avoid official subjects at social functions; don't spend the evening "talking shop" in a tight little knot.

*Leaving a function* before the guest of honor is as improper in military circles as it is in civilian. By the same token, it is not normally polite to leave before the commanding officer—or the senior officer present.

### Presents

It is customary, particularly in peacetime units, to give inscribed wedding presents and baby cups. This is an agreeable practice if it does not work a financial hardship.

A suitable gift—usually an item of sterling silver—can be obtained at a reasonable price if the purchasing is in the hands of a person of good taste and some experience. (It's best to tap one of the wives for this mission.)

Remember, however, that regulations specifically prohibit gifts to a superior officer or his family.

### Flower Funds

Many organizations establish a fund from which to buy flowers on appropriate occasions in the name of the officers. The adjutant is the logical candidate to handle this fund. Periodically he will assess officers a nominal amount to refill his fund's coffers.

### Tipping or Removing the Hat Is Taboo

The civilian practice of tipping one's hat to a lady, or of standing cap in hand in the presence of a lady, is not proper for an officer (or enlisted man) in uniform.

This custom of not removing the uniform hat when out of doors is universal and very old. It can be the cause of some embarrassment to regular officers during mobilization since the civilian habit of whipping off one's headdress is understandably expected.

### Addressing Junior Officers Socially as "Mister"

It used to be that Army lieutenants were addressed socially (and sometimes in oral official communications) as "Mister." This practice is observed these days only by a few "wives of the Old Army."

The Navy still clings to the old traditions and frowns on addressing officers below the rank of Commander by their titles. When speaking—socially *or* officially—to naval officers below the rank of Commander you should use "Mister."

### Swords at the Military Wedding

At some military weddings the bridegroom, best man and ushers (if they are officers) will wear swords in the tradition of the Old Army (the swords having been, in all probability, borrowed for the occasion).

The bride will cut the wedding cake with her husband's sword— or with the sword of one of his or her forebears. (It is "poor form" and a little silly to use a sword that has no legitimate family connection.) A practical note here: Be certain that the sword is well cleaned of cake and frosting before it is re-sheathed.

Outside the church an arch of crossed swords may be formed for the bride and groom to pass under.

The traditional arch of swords at military weddings may well be a vestige of the day when the groom had to take elaborate precautions to protect his bride from capture by her kinsmen or by soreheaded ex-beaux.

In the old days a "best man" was literally that: a friend the groom picked to take charge of "security measures." As an additional safety precaution, weddings were frequently held at night.

"At the Swedish church of Husaby," writes Radford, "long lances, which were fitted with sockets for torches, were kept. These were used by the groomsmen for possible defense and also to illuminate the night wedding ceremony."

An occasional innovator comes up with the suggestion that the ushers use swagger sticks, rifles, or bayonets to symbolize the arch of swords. This is considered poor taste. The only proper substitute for the sword arch is to have ushers stand at attention facing each other in two ranks while the bride and groom leave the church.

An arch of swords is logically out of the question when the bridegroom and ushers are not commissioned officers. (What is proper when the bride is a commissioned officer and the groom a civilian? That's a "good question.")

### Bridal Procession

The military wedding used to be quite a distinctive, colorful and delightful affair. Part of the color has been lost with the obsolescence of the saber. Much of the rest went with the caisson. But the old traditions have survived on many posts—with borrowed swords for the ushers and jeeps or armored cars for the caisson. There is no reason why the old customs connected with honoring the officer's bride cannot be more widely revived.

The bride who once was escorted from the chapel with her groom on an artillery caisson may now be seen off on a gaily decorated jeep, tank or armored car.

An officer returning to his outfit with his bride may be met at the gate to the post with a caparisoned vehicle of some sort and driven in the convoy of his friends, amid the tooting of horns or the music of the unit band, for an inaugural tour of the post. The procession may stop at the Officers' Club for a brief welcoming party.

A welcoming committee may have prepared the quarters of the new couple—if they are in the happy position of having quarters available.

### New Arrivals Should Be Made Welcome

The custom of seeing that the newcomer is well received is another that has roots in practical necessity. The Army family may well make as many moves in five years as the average civilian family makes in two generations. At best it is an expensive and trying experience, but the burden can be eased tremendously if the new arrival is met with efficient, courteous and hospitable treatment.

An officer should look on all brother officers as members of the military "family." Like members of your own family, it will not always be convenient to take care of some distant cousin and his three screaming brats while he finds a place to live. But it's one of the things decent people do.

## Some Tips for the Ladies

It is improper for a woman to wear items of military insignia as jewelry. You will see it done, but it is actually prohibited by law.

Wearing a soldier's hat is very cute in a beer joint, but is more in character for a floozie than a lady.

A gal who is really in the know militarily will be careful not to get her hands on metal insignia or ornaments. If she happens to be associating with soldiers who take some pride in their appearance, she will leave finger marks which they will have to take some pains to remove. Captains' and lieutenants' bars on the shoulder are particularly vulnerable at dances.

Asking for an explanation of a soldier's decorations is taboo in the British Army. (You're supposed to know.) A soldier would probably be happy to explain his decorations if he felt somebody *really* wanted to know what they were. But he has long since ceased to be amused by such conversational gambits as "Now, how did you get *that* cute little one—[pointing fatuously to the Good-Conduct Medal]—did you sink an enemy battleship?"

Use your head about mixing officers and enlisted men at social functions. There are many times when this is completely proper—such as when family relationships or old friendships are involved. However, remember that it is "not done" as a matter of general practice.

# Appendix A

*Fourragères* and Aiguillettes

by

C. C. SODEN

From a heretofore unpublished MS. kindly furnished by the author

Away back in Marlborough's time the question of fodder for all mounted units was no great problem, such horse feed being purchased from farmers, etc., able to supply same. In consequence of this it was but rarely necessary for a regiment to carry along a reserve supply. This, however, applied only to the peacetime routine of the army in England.

Naturally enough when on active service abroad a very different state of affairs prevailed, the troops operating in enemy country usually having to resort to open looting of homes and granaries in order to obtain food both for themselves and for the horses.

Having this in mind, Marlborough, before he took his army over to the Low Countries, caused each of his Cavalrymen to be furnished with a canvas bag which was attached by a snap hook to a cord worn over the right shoulder.

These bags were much larger and more cumbersome than the regulation type used in peacetime and when not in use were strapped over the blanket on the back of the saddle. The cord referred to was, for convenience' sake, looped up and worn behind the right shoulder, being kept in place by a metal hook on the jacket.

Each morning a number of men were detailed for the duty of

scouring the countryside in search of the required food supplies. It
naturally followed that their operations were attended by varying
degrees of success, some returning with only a small amount and
others with their bags filled to bursting point. The latter, by the way,
were always rewarded with a tot of rum or mug of ale.

In the French Army any regiment which gained distinction in
action against an enemy was awarded the semi-official name of
*Feuragère* in recognition of the feat.

Thus it came about that the British soldiers' aptitude for applying
enemy terms in an ironical manner in regard to their own activities
resulted in the name *Feuragère* being bestowed on any man, or
party of men, who had achieved outstanding success in the matter
of looting food supplies from the civilian population in enemy
territory.

Though regarded at the time as merely a nickname soon to be
forgotten, the name nevertheless stuck and, in the corrupted form
of "forager," became adopted as a word in the English language.
Indeed, a few short years later when a small cap intended for "Un-
dress" purposes was issued it was officially named a "forage" cap
and by this name has passed down through the years to the present
day.

The cord to which the original food bag was attached was, in the
case of the ordinary trooper, quite a plain affair featuring no ornamentation whatever. When the Army returned to England after the
war these were replaced by ones a little more decorative, and when
not used to carry the bag, were still worn in the manner already
described. Officers who had hitherto not worn these cords now also
adopted them but for purely ornamental purposes, theirs consisting
of a cord plaited along its whole length.

Like the ordinary Troopers' they were worn over the back of the
shoulder, being held in place by a button or sometimes a fancy
"toggle" sewn on the jacket. At first the cords were pipeclayed but
were later replaced by silk ones, each branch of the mounted troops
such as Artillery, "Light" and "Heavy" Cavalry having a distinguishing color. Another innovation consisted of the adoption of
different types of plaiting and thickness according to the officer's
rank, the latter having previously only been indicated by varying
amount of braid on sleeve cuffs and pocket flaps. Around 1730 we

find further developments in the shape of metal spikes or "aiguilles" attached to the ends of the cords, the latter now being held in position on the shoulder by means of a fringed portion of braid attached to the cords, this of course being in its turn the origin of the epaulette.

In the case of high-ranking officers the loops were worn, not at the back, but suspended from the center of the shoulder, the plaited cords thus falling down over the front as well as the back of the jacket.

In 1735 the colored silk cord was suspended by gold bullion for the Cavalry and silver for the Infantry, who had now taken to wearing them.

In the case of Staff Officers the cords, etc., were, a short time later, carried right across the breast, the long spiked ends being attached to either a hook beneath the collar or a button of the jacket.

# Appendix B

**Critical Dates in Military Evolution**

ca. 400  Beginning of the Dark Ages. Military knowledge dies along with other forms of learning.

ca. 500  Stirrup appears in Europe (undoubtedly from Asia). This simple device—along with the tree saddle—enables the man on horseback to start his rise to battlefield supremacy. At Hastings (1066) the military horseman (in Europe) has "arrived." During the feudal period he is unbeatable by foot troops.

ca. 1300  Gunpowder starts being widely used. Almost a century is to pass, however, before it becomes really significant in combat.

1346  English yeomen with longbows defeat armored French knights at Crécy to confirm the return of the foot soldier to battlefield supremacy after an absence of almost ten centuries. Swiss herdsmen, armed with modified farm implements (pikes, halberds, etc.), had shown at Morgarten in 1315 that they had another effective way of bringing Sir Knight down off his high horse and busting him open like a lobster. When Swiss and English mercenaries teamed up they were the death of chivalry.

ca. 1500  About the time of the discovery of America, German mercenaries known as *Landsknechte* ("land knights") and *Reiter* ("riders") developed tactics and organization on which all other European armies soon modeled themselves. Their influence remains today.

1645    "New Model Army" raised by Oliver Cromwell. By studying classical armies of Greece and Rome and making sweeping reforms in existing military methods, he creates an unbeatable army along "modern" lines.

1660    British Regular Army born after Restoration of Charles II. This is a critical date in British military traditions, just as 1784 is in our Army.

1775    American Regular Army born (June 14).

1784    American Regular Army abolished by Congress except for the eighty-man detail retained to guard Revolutionary War supplies. Thus the link was broken between our present-day Army and the Continental Army. Battery D, Fifth F. A. Battalion, by virtue of a rather tenuous lineage to the eighty-man guard detail, is the only exception.

1800    The division is used by Napoleon as a new type of tactical organization. Until then the battalion had been the largest tactical unit—the regiment had been purely administrative.

ca. 1861    Traditional "parade ground" tactics shown during American Civil War to be obsolete. Chief reason: the new *minié* ("minnie") bullet, a French invention, made rifle fire more effective. Fancy uniforms, close-order drill, "colors" and other vestiges of medieval warfare were relegated to the parade ground.

1903    Airplane invented by the Wright brothers.

1945    Atom bomb ushers in a new era of warfare.

# Appendix C

### An Explanation of Some Confusing Terms

The term "United States Army" is now used in its literal sense. It is no longer restricted to the *Regular Army,* except in reference to old statutes in which the term was specifically limited to the Regular Army. Use of the term "Army of the United States" is officially discouraged.

### What Is a "Component"?

Our Army is divided into three "components": the Regular Army; the National Guard; and the Organized Reserve Corps. The last two (NG and ORC) are also known as the "civilian components."

### "Branches"

The "Branches of the Army" are:

*Basic Branches*

Adjutant General's Corps
Armor
Artillery
Chemical Corps
Corps of Engineers
Finance Corps
Infantry
Military Police Corps

168

Ordnance Corps
Quartermaster Corps
Signal Corps
Transportation

*Special Branches*

Chaplains
Judge Advocate General's Corps
Army Medical Service, which consists of
    Medical Corps
    Dental Corps
    Veterinary Corps
    Medical Service Corps
    Army Nurse Corps
    Women's Medical Specialist Corps

*Other Branches*

The following are defined as branches to which only Reserve personnel not on active duty may be assigned:

Army Security
Military Intelligence
Staff Specialist
Civil Affairs/Military Government

## "Arms" and "Services"

The "Branches of the Army" may be classified into "arms," "administrative services," and "technical services."

The official dictionary (SR 320-5-1) defines an "arm" as a "branch of the Army, such as Infantry, Armored Cavalry, or Artillery, the primary function of which is combat." The term "combat arm" is also used to mean the same thing. The Corps of Engineers and Signal Corps, both of which furnish close combat support in addition to performing rear-area functions, are generally considered to be "arms" as well as "services."

Branches classified as *Administrative Services* are the Adjutant General's Corps, Chaplains, and the Military Police Corps.

Branches which compose the *Technical Services* are the Army

Medical Service (which is composed of six corps), Chemical Corps, Corps of Engineers, Ordnance Corps, Quartermaster Corps, Signal Corps and Transportation Corps.

## IG's and WAC's

The Inspector General does not have a branch. He is "detailed" for the office and is assisted Army-wide by other officers who are similarly detailed for limited periods of time. The Army's first IG, incidentally, was Baron von Steuben.

Members of the Women's Army Corps (established May 14, 1942, as the Women's *Auxiliary* Army Corps) are also in a different status from the organizations we have been discussing. (*Vive la différence!*) They do not constitute a branch or a component, but are "detailed" to certain of the branches.

## Sources

For readers who find that some of this information conflicts with previous understanding, let me cite AR 320-5 and SR 320-5-1. Changes are constantly being made, particularly in the official names of the branches.

# Bibliography

"I am profoundly suspicious of almost all bibliographies," writes A. G. Macdonell at the end of his fine *Napoleon and His Marshals.* "Nothing is easier than to hire someone to visit the British Museum [or the Library of Congress] and make a most impressive list of authorities, which will persuade the non-suspecting that the author is a monument of erudition and laboriousness."

Although I share the above attitude completely, this book would be incomplete without a list of main sources. Please keep in mind that this is not a bibliography of military history in general, but one restricted to the field of military *customs* and *traditions.*[1]

PART I: STANDARD REFERENCES ON MILITARY ORIGINS

Ashdown, Charles H., *British and Foreign Arms and Armor,* London, 1909. A one-volume work, highly illustrated; recommended.

Dodge, Lt. Col. Theodore A., *Napoleon,* Boston and New York, 1904, 4 vols. By far the most prolific of American military writers— which, I'm afraid, is like being the giant in a tribe of pigmies!— Colonel Dodge is noted for his ambitious Great Captains Series which includes *Alexander, Hannibal, Caesar, Gustavus Adolphus,* etc. He has dealt exhaustively with the history of the art of war and, although not universally esteemed as an authority, is "required reading" for real military scholars.

---

[1] *A Guide to the Writing of American Military History,* Department of the Army, 1950, includes an extensive bibliography of source material on American military history. Available from the Government Printing Office.

Ffoulkes, Charles, *Arms and Armament,* London, 1945. A brief but very thorough coverage by a real authority. Valuable bibliography. Recommended.

Fortescue, Sir John W., *A History of the British Army,* London and New York, 1899, 13 volumes of text plus 6 volumes of maps. First volume is extremely valuable for information on early military origins in Europe. By long odds my most valuable source. Highly recommended.

———— *The Empire and the Army,* London, 1928. A one-volume "popularization" of his longer work. Recommended.

Foster, Col. Hubert, *Organization: How Armies Are Formed for War,* London, 1913. Despite its unpromising title, this book is a gold mine of military lore. In tracing the evolution of army organization, Foster gives a concise and scholarly account of military developments since the sixteenth century. Highly recommended.

Froissart's *Chronicles.* Written in the fourteenth century, this source has contributed heavily to subsequent writings on war in the Middle Ages. Most editions now in print are children's versions. One such is in the "Everyman's Library" series, London and New York, 1930.

Grose's *Military Antiquities,* 1786. Definitely a "rare book," this is a two-volume, highly illustrated work which—like Froissart—is much quoted in almost all more recent works on military history and customs. It is principally drawn on for pictures of ancient "engines of war"—such as the "Petard."

Hewitt, John, *Ancient Armour and Weapons in Europe,* London, 1860, 3 vols. A prime source of material through the seventeenth century. Valuable illustrations from old manuscripts and monuments. Recommended for specialists.

Hime, Lt. Col. Henry W. L., *The Origin of Artillery,* London, 1915. A thorough treatment of the subject. Interesting and readable despite its frightful erudition: many notes in Greek, a chapter in Latin, a footnote in Arabic!

James, Charles, *A Universal Military Dictionary,* London, 1802; Fourth Edition, 1816. Although frequently cited by military writers, I found James unrewarding and inaccurate. Valuable as the "Officers' Guide" of his period.

Moss, Col. James A., *Officers' Manual* (Banta Pub. Co., Menasha, Wisc.), 1913. This was the U. S. Army officers' "bible" until eclipsed in recent years by the *Officers' Guide* (Military Service Publishing Co., Harrisburg, Penna.).

———— *Origin and Significance of Military Customs,* Banta, 1917. A meager work which was incorporated in later editions of Moss's *Officers' Manual.*

Oman, Sir Charles, *The Art of War in the Middle Ages.* This is *the* standard work on the subject. First published as an essay in 1884, it was expanded into two volumes in 1924. A revised, one-volume version, edited by John H. Beeler, was published by the Cornell University Press in 1953. Recommended.

Powell, Col. James W., *Customs of the Service,* Kansas City, 1905. An "officers' guide," devoted primarily to advice and little preachments on how to perform various normal military duties. Some useful historical data (e.g., badges of Civil War and Spanish-American War units).

Royal Prussian War Office, *German Military Uniforms at the International Exhibition in Paris in 1900.* This small, 116-page book (in English) gives a brief and thoroughly authentic coverage of German uniforms from their beginning in 1680 until 1863. It includes eighty-three photos of life-size figures in uniform. It is apparent that several modern authors have drawn heavily on this obscure source.

Vegetius, *Military Institutions of the Romans,* Harrisburg, Penna., 1944. This is a modern edition of a book that has been a classic since the fall of Rome.

Wyllie, Col. (later B.G.) Robert E., *Orders, Decorations and Insignia,* New York, 1921. Includes "the history and romance of their origin." Interesting but, some authorities tell me, not accurate.

### Part II: Current Books

Most of the books listed above are, unfortunately, hard to find. The following, if not still in print, are accessible.

Colby, Col. Elbridge, *Army Talk,* Princeton, 1942. A rich source.

Department of the Army, *The Army Almanac,* Government

Printing Office (GPO), 1950. "A book of facts concerning the Army," it is worth the price of $3.

────── *The Army Lineage Book: Vol. II, Infantry*, GPO, 1953, $2. In 860 pages, this paperback book gives the "traditions, honors, and devices" of all U. S. infantry regiments and separate battalions. Valuable reference for official descriptions and illustrations of insignia and coats of arms, for official lineages, campaign streamers, decorations and published histories for each unit. Beyond the above records, it gives no history or traditions. A sixty-one-page "History of the Organization of United States Infantry," by John K. Mahon, provides a valuable introduction. (Other volumes of this series are "in preparation.")

────── *The Medal of Honor*, GPO, 1948. A history of this and other U. S. decorations that is well written and interesting. Includes available pictures of MH winners.

────── *Selected Quotations, U. S. Military Leaders, 1955*. Mimeographed.

────── *The Soldier's Guide* (Field Manual 21-13), GPO, 1952 (55¢). A sixty-four-page chapter on "History and Achievement of Our Army," it is the best popular coverage I have found. Recommended.

Department of Defense, *The Armed Forces Officer*, GPO, 1950. Although officially anonymous, this was written by S. L. A. Marshall (author of *Men Against Fire, The River and the Gauntlet, Bastogne*, etc.). Useful as the official statement of Army, Navy and Air Force "customs of the Service."

Downey, Fairfax D., *Indian Fighting Army*, New York, 1941. Recommended.

────── *Mascots*, New York, 1954. (Juvenile.) Recommended.

Earle, Edward Mead (ed.), *Makers of Modern Strategy*, Princeton, 1952. Section I, "The Origins of Modern War," was particularly useful.

Edwards, Major T. J., *Military Customs* (Gale & Polden, Aldershot, England), 1950. The only other modern book in English I have found on this subject. Deals primarily with customs of the colorful and tradition-conscious British Army, from whom so many of our own customs stem. Recommended.

Field, Colonel Cyril, *Old Times Under Arms: A Military Garner,* London, 1939. As its title indicates, this (in the words of its author) is a collection of "odds and ends connected with the profession of arms which I have picked up and accumulated in the course of many years of more or less casual research in very varied directions." Recommended.

Ganoe, Colonel W. A., *The History of the United States Army,* New York, 1932. The original book in this field and still the standard work. Not rewarding, however, as a source of Army "color."

——— *Soldiers Unmasked,* Hartford, 1935. A series of radio talks explaining the soldier to the general public. Candid and readable.

Jacobs, James Ripley, *The Beginning of the U. S. Army, 1783–1812,* Princeton, 1947. Like Ganoe, strictly "historical."

Laver, James, *British Military Uniforms,* London, 1948. A small ("King Penguin") book, illustrated with color plates, by an authority. Recommended.

Lawson, Cecil C. P., *The Uniforms of the British Army,* London, 1940. Although there are many books on this subject, this two-volume, thoroughly illustrated work is outstanding.

Lovette, Lt. Cmdr. Leland P., *Naval Customs, Traditions and Usage,* Annapolis, 1934. A monumental work which contains some information on Army customs and military origins. Essentially a Naval "officers' guide."

Mitchell, Colonel William A., *Outlines of the World's Military History,* Harrisburg, Pennsylvania, Military Service Publishing Company, 1935. A good source of military origins. Recommended.

National Geographic Society, *Insignia and Decorations of the U. S. Armed Forces,* Washington, 1944. Aside from being the only book covering this field, it is also valuable for its historical data. 2,476 reproductions in color.

Spaulding, Colonel Oliver L., *The United States Army in War and Peace,* New York, 1937. A standard work.

Spaulding, Col. Oliver L.; Hoffman, Capt. Nickerson; and Wright, Col. John W.; *Warfare: A Study of Military Methods from the Earliest Times,* Washington, 1937. This is a scholarly one-volume survey. Includes valuable bibliographies. Highly recommended.

Stradling, Group Captain A. H., *Customs of the Services* (Gale & Polden, Aldershot, England), 1949. A thin primer of British "service etiquette." Includes a reprint of the "Tomes Lecture" of 1925 (see footnote, page 24).

Tunis, Edwin, *Weapons, A Pictorial History* (World, Cleveland and New York), 1954. An outstanding book on the evolution of weapons. Recommended.

Wintringham, Thomas H., *The Story of Weapons and Tactics from Troy to Stalingrad,* Boston, 1943. Good.